THE
ROTISSERIE
GRILLING
COOKBOOK

THE ROTISSERIE GRILLING COOKBOOK

SUREFIRE RECIPES & FOOLPROOF TECHNIQUES

Derrick Riches & Sabrina Baksh

HARVARD COMMON PRESS

© 2017 Quarto Publishing Group USA Inc.
Text © 2017 Derrick Riches and Sabrina Baksh

First Published in 2017 by The Harvard Common Press, an imprint of The Quarto Group,
100 Cummings Center, Suite 265-D, Beverly, MA 01915, USA.
T (978) 282-9590 F (978) 283-2742 QuartoKnows.com

The Harvard Common Press titles are also available at discount for retail, wholesale, promotional, and bulk purchase. For details, contact the Special Sales Manager by email at specialsales@quarto.com or by mail at The Quarto Group, Attn: Special Sales Manager, 100 Cummings Center, Suite 265-D, Beverly, MA 01915, USA.

ISBN: 978-1-55832-873-0

Digital edition published in 2017

Library of Congress Cataloging-in-Publication Data

Names: Riches, Derrick, author. | Baksh, Sabrina, author.
Title: The rotisserie grilling cookbook : surefire recipes and foolproof
   techniques / Derrick Riches and Sabrina Baksh.
Description: Digital edition. | Beverly, Massachusetts : Harvard Common
   Press, an imprint of Quarto Publishing Group USA, Inc., [2017] | Includes
   index.
Identifiers: LCCN 2017018610 | ISBN 9781558328730
Subjects: LCSH: Barbecuing. | Marinades. | Cooking. | LCGFT: Cookbooks.
Classification: LCC TX840.B3 R54 2017 | DDC 641.7/6--dc23 LC record available at https://lccn.loc.gov/2017018610

Photography: Mark Maziarz Photography except pages 4, 10, 16, 17, 18, 20, 51, 53, 58, 62, 65, 91, 101, 109, and 198, courtesy of Shutterstock

CONTENTS

BASIC EQUIPMENT AND TECHNIQUES FOR ROTISSERIE GRILLING

In our twenty years of writing about barbecue and grilling, one of the most frequent questions we hear is, why the rotisserie? Almost all gas grills have a rotisserie option and many charcoal grills have rotisserie accessories available. Although these items are commonly available, many people are still hesitant to think of them as an important extension of their regular grilling practices. This is truly a shame.

Grills purchased straight from the showroom floor are perfect for cooking burgers, steaks, hot dogs, and kebabs, but when it comes to roasts and whole chickens, they often struggle. To properly grill a steak requires a high, direct heat. The steak sits over the fire. The surface browns and develops a crust quickly, while the interior can achieve any level of desired doneness. Steaks are relatively thin and cook fast. A large roast or whole chicken, on the other hand, requires slower roasting to achieve perfection. Cooked over high heat, these meats will char on the exterior before the center has a chance to reach an appropriate temperature.

To cook large pieces of meat requires indirect grilling coupled with low heat. Simply stated, indirect grilling is exactly what it sounds like: The heat is to the side of the food and not directly underneath. Depending on the size of the grill in question, this can be done relatively easily, but it will still require a lot of turning. Turning over. Turning around. Turning back. Lots of movement to achieve an even and complete cooking. The rotisserie, however, does all of the turning and so much more. It allows you to cook larger cuts of meat than you can by direct-heat grilling, but without as much fuss as indirect grilling requires.

A proper rotisserie rotates at a speed that keeps the juices from dripping excessively and allows them to roll around the surface of foods. This is why there are sometimes stripes running around rotisserie chickens or roasts. These natural juices baste the meat continually, which reduces drying and increases flavor.

The constant rotation also reduces the likelihood of burning. No one side of the food is exposed to the heat long enough to cause charring. It gets hot and then moves on. This means that rotisserie cooking is faster and easier than simply placing large cuts of meat on the cooking grates. It requires less monitoring and a shorter cooking time because the grill can be operated at a higher temperature. What results is an evenly cooked roast, whole bird, or whatever main or side dish you choose to prepare.

While food on a rotisserie is self-basted, the constant turning motion makes it easier to add an extra baste as it cooks. This means flavors can be layered throughout the grilling process without having to pick up a pair of tongs or doing much more than simply lifting the lid and painting on a baste. And because the baste stays on the food as it turns, less is needed and the food absorbs more of its flavor.

GRILL TYPES: GAS VERSUS INFRARED VERSUS CHARCOAL

Most large grills can do rotisserie cooking. At its most basic level, it is simply a dry roasting method of cooking. The difference is that the food is suspended and is in constant motion. The process is not all that dissimilar from placing a roast or chicken on a rack in the oven to cook. Out on the grill, the roasting environment is drier, which is optimal, because a wet roasting method reduces the browning on the surface; the dry environment is what gives us the crusty surface or bite through skin that we are looking for. It is this dry, hot environment that is best for roasting.

The type of grill being used will also make a difference. Gas grills are more convenient, while charcoal grills produce a more authentic, smoky flavor. Charcoal grills have the driest cooking environment and propane grills the wettest, though by "wet" we are talking about a relative amount of moisture. This has to do with the water created during combustion. When something burns, it produces water vapor. Propane produces quite a lot, natural gas a little less, and charcoal even less than that. This is one of the reasons that people can sometimes tell the difference between foods cooked over gas versus foods cooked over live coals.

A drier roasting environment does not mean a drier piece of meat. Our recipes are designed to work on all types of grills and no adjustments should be necessary. However, we believe that it is important for people to understand the differences and be prepared to use their specific grill to its maximum capability. Of course, if you are reading this book, you probably already own the grill you will be using, but someday you might be shopping for a new one and understanding these differences might come in handy.

One of the challenges of writing a grilling cookbook is that there is no way we can know what type of grill you are using and under what circumstances. There are many variables in the kinds of fire, grill shape, fuel source, and size of different types of grills. The times and heat used in this book are more a guide than a specific rule. Your grill will cook differently than the grills we used to test these recipes. Add to this wind, air temperature, altitude, and all the other variables that come with outdoor cooking, and the simple truth is that you are going to have to adjust temperatures and times based on your environment and experience. While rotisserie cooking is forgiving, flare-ups are possible, charcoal fires can die, and the wind can move heat from one end of a grill to the other. Do not consider this a discouragement, but part of the outdoor cooking experience, which of course, we all enjoy.

Gas Grills

Gas grills are the most appliance-like of all outdoor cooking equipment. There are knobs for temperature control that allow heat to be adjusted quickly and easily. The lid holds in enough heat for proper convection and the burners are generally predictable. As long as the fuel does not run out, it will keep going strong under almost all conditions.

Ideally, a gas grill should be large enough to place the food in the center with heat on either side. If you are working with a smaller three-burner grill, consider the length of the food being cooked and how well the gas grill will accommodate the size of the item. Small, two-burner grills can handle a rotisserie, but the heat will be much more direct, so temperature adjustments will need to be made. A drip pan is necessary to deflect the direct heat away from the food. In this situation, the burners should be adjusted to a slightly lower temperature than the recipe calls for.

The control knobs on the gas grill are to be taken at face value. So when we say medium-high heat, the burners being used should be adjusted to that position on the dial. Learning how your grill works is an important skill, so monitoring food as it cooks and adjusting accordingly is up to you. It is your grill, and while we are here to guide you through the process, you are in control.

Start by reading your grill's user manual for rotisserie cooking. This will provide all the specifics necessary for proper placement and usage of your rotisserie unit. In general, these instructions are simple. If using a propane grill, make certain that there is sufficient fuel. The recipes in this book range in cooking times from as little as 30 minutes to up to 6 hours. We always recommend a second, full propane tank be kept on hand to change out if necessary. If the fuel runs low while preparing one of our recipes, there will not be time to run out and purchase a fuel tank without causing serious consequences to the food being prepared.

Infrared Rotisserie Burners

If your grill is equipped with a rear-mounted rotisserie burner (typically infrared, but the same rules apply to standard rotisserie burners), then the cooking mechanics will work a little differently. As we said earlier, read the manufacturer's user manual before using the grill and its rotisserie system.

The biggest difference of using a rear-mounted rotisserie burner is simply the location of the heat source. Because drippings will not reach the burners, the chances of a flare-up or grease fire are remote at best. This does not mean that a drip pan is not a good idea. Those drippings, left inside the grill, will cause a substantial fire the next time the main burners are lit, so again, always use a drip pan and keep your grill clean and ready to use next time.

Rotisserie burners provide even heat and are generally wide enough to accommodate any food item. It is important that the burner overlaps the food by at least an inch or two (2.5 to 5 cm) on each side. Centering foods relative to the burner will ensure even cooking. These burners can be adjusted to provide a wide range of heat, though low-temperature cooking may be harder to achieve with infrared. There must be a minimum of 2 to 3 inches (5 to 7.5 cm) between the food and the burner at all times.

Some grills equipped with infrared rotisserie burners recommend using the burner as little as 20 minutes before switching to the main burners to finish off with indirect heat. Rotisserie burners can be hot and may cause burning of the surface before the food has finished cooking. This is certainly an issue with poultry, which must be cooked to a higher internal temperature than most roasts.

Charcoal Grills

Charcoal grills offer the best versatility for rotisserie cooking. Although gas grills are more convenient for this process, charcoal grills actually have a drier cooking environment and are perfect for roasting; with a little practice, you can achieve a wider range of temperature control, from very low to very high. The problem with many charcoal grills is that they do not offer a rotisserie option. The various versions of the 22-inch (56 cm) Weber Charcoal Kettle Grill (and most 22-inch [56 cm] round charcoal grills) have an available rotisserie option. Now there is a rotisserie unit available that will fit any 18-inch (45.7 cm) Kamado-style grill. Depending on the type of charcoal grill you have, there might not be an available unit. Of course, you have this book, so you probably have a rotisserie unit for your charcoal grill already.

When using a charcoal grill, the fire needs to be built on the side of the grill parallel to the rotisserie rod in such a way that the fire will not be directly under the food. Although the charcoal fire can be on both sides of the grill, temperature control will be easier if one fire is made. To keep the coals in place, use a deep aluminum drip pan under the food, with the fire pushed to one side of the pan. Additional charcoal can be easily added as necessary.

With kettle-style charcoal grills, it is important to control the airflow through the grill so that heat and smoke pass over the food and not around it. Most of these grills have a top vent to one side of the handle, and you can direct airflow by turning the lid so that the vent is on the opposite side of the grill relative to the fire.

With Kamado-style grills, it is best to use the grill's deflector plate (sometimes known as a plate setter) to ensure indirect cooking and prevent burning. Placing a drip pan onto the deflector will help keep the grill clean and prevent drips from reaching the fire. Make sure that you have tested the temperature control on this style of grill, because they can easily reach temperatures over 700°F (370°C). The manufacturer's user manual outlines vent control and because there can be a small learning curve, practice a bit before cooking something expensive for company. Remember, with Kamado-style grills, it is much easier to bring the temperature up than to bring it down. Start with the vents closed to limit the airflow and bring the heat up slowly to the desired cooking temperature.

GRILL TEMPERATURES

Most modern grills come equipped with a temperature gauge built into the lid. These are a good guide but are not accurate enough to rely on. The truth is no grill, gas or charcoal, works like your indoor oven. Temperatures are much more general. Be ready to make adjustments to your grill as you cook, trying to work toward the cooking times that we recommend. However, remember that these times are a general guide as well. Be attentive, and with a little practice you will easily master controlling your grill's cooking temperature. Here are the heat terms that we use in the book:

High heat means as hot as your grill will get. With gas grills, this is much more controllable, provided that you are not experiencing a serious flare-up. For charcoal, "high heat" refers to the hottest temperature the grill will reach in a controlled manner with the lid in place. Charcoal grills can reach much higher temperatures than gas grills, so make sure that your charcoal fire is controlled and in the appropriate range. Any cooking temperature between 450°F and 550°F (232°C and 288°C) is considered high heat. If you cannot hold your hand over the fire for at least one second, this is a high temperature.

Medium-high heat falls in the temperature range between 350°F and 400°F (177°C and 204°C). You should be able to hold your hand directly over the heat for one to two seconds comfortably. Medium-high heat is a faster roasting temperature for rotisserie cooking and is used for items that require a caramelized surface.

Medium heat is any temperature around 350°F (177°C). You should be able to hold your hand over it for a count of three seconds before it gets too hot (please don't burn yourself). Medium heat is a good slow-roasting temperature for many rotisserie items. This temperature is gentle on meats, particularly poultry, and produces a tender and juicy bird without any excessive drying during the cooking process.

MAKING SMOKE

Smoke flavor can be added to any food cooked on an outdoor rotisserie. What we have found over the years is that some people prefer smokiness to their foods, while others find it undesirable. Some of our recipes are built around this flavor profile and we recommend the addition of smoke to achieve the proper results. However, it is entirely up to you to do so.

Charcoal grills impart some smoke flavor while gas grills do not. On a charcoal unit, adding smoke is very easy. Burning most modern charcoal produces a small amount of smoke flavor. When charcoal burns hot, it produces very little smoke. To increase this, add hardwood chunks (not chips) to the burning fire once the food is in place. Add as much or as little as you deem appropriate. To produce a strong smoke flavor, it is best to add it at the very beginning of the cooking process and again at the halfway mark. Keep in mind that foods absorb less smoke the longer they cook.

When it comes to gas grills, adding smoke is a little trickier. Charcoal grills work by limiting airflow, so any smoke produced is held inside the grill longer. Gas grills are like heat pumps, pushing hot air through the grill quickly. Any smoke made inside a gas grill will quickly vent out, so it needs to travel over the food as directly as possible and in an indirect cooking situation. This is not so easy to accomplish because most of the smoke will exit the grill away from the food.

Even though gas grills will not impart the same level of smoke flavor as charcoal grills do, a light smoke flavor can be added with relative ease. On the market are a number of "smoker boxes" that can be used with gas grills, and they work fairly well. However, it is easy to make "smoke bombs" by wrapping hardwood chunks in aluminum foil. Make the foil packet loose so that there is space inside the packet for combustion and airflow. Puncture several holes in the foil on all sides. For this packet to produce smoke, it must be heated to the combustion point of wood, or around 450°F (232°C). Once it starts producing a strong smoke, the packet should keep burning until all the wood is burned away. To get the packet up to full heat, place it as close to a main grill burner as possible and set that burner on high. This can be done once the food is on the rotisserie and cooking. It will take about 10 minutes for the packet to begin producing smoke. Once it does, adjust the burner to the desired cooking temperature, move the packet directly under the food, and keep the lid closed for as long as smoke is being produced. A little practice with this method will go a long way toward success. We recommend trying this smoke-making process on the grill without food to get the hang of it. Once food is on the grill there is little time for experimenting.

When selecting wood for making smoke, look for hardwood chunks that are 1 to 2 inches (2.5 to 5 cm) in size and labeled for cooking. Treated, stained, or painted wood contains toxic chemicals that are not only undesirable in flavor but also dangerous to your health.

Hardwoods used for smoking are available in a wide range of flavors. They range from strong to mild flavor and can be grouped based on their strength.

- Mesquite has a heavy and acidic flavor that can easily impart a very strong smoke. We recommend using this wood very sparingly.

- Hickory is a favorite of Southern barbecue, but also contains a strong flavor. This is a great wood for pork and dense roasts. Try this wood in small amounts until you have a good grasp of the flavor it will provide.

- Oak is one of the most popular of all smoking woods. It has a mild but distinctive flavor and works very well with most foods.

- Fruitwoods are a large category of hardwood, ranging from apple and cherry to pecan and walnut. These woods have a mild flavor and are perfect for the person who just wants a hint of smokiness. These woods are recommended for all types of poultry.

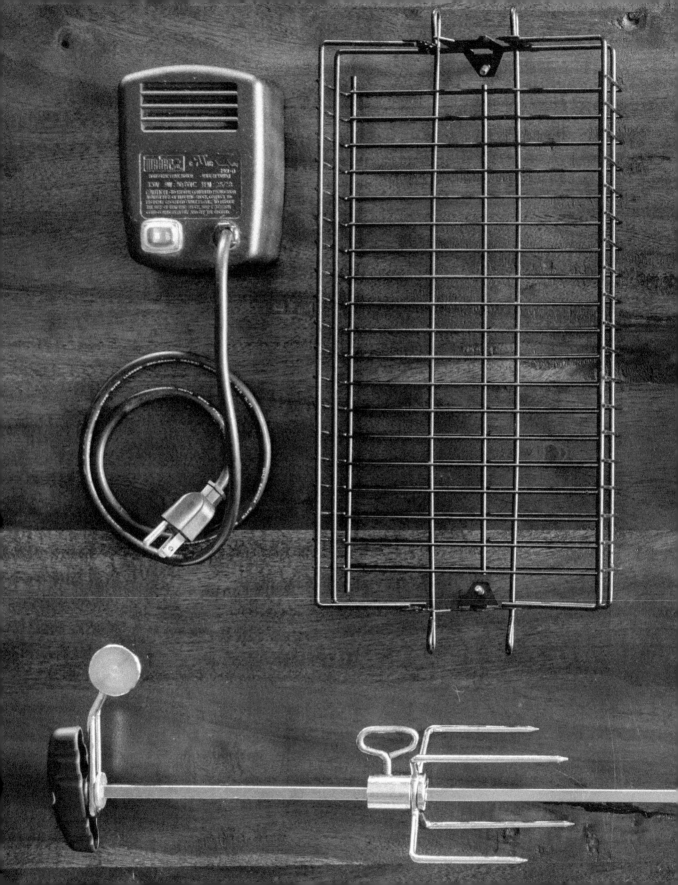

Rotisserie Units

All rotisserie systems work with the cooking grates removed. The typical rotisserie system is rated to handle between 15 and 20 pounds (6.8 and 9 kg) of food. There are grills with rotisserie systems that can handle up to 100 pounds (45.4 kg), but typically they are only on the most expensive of gas grills. Your manual will tell you how much the motor on your rotisserie system can handle. We do not recommend exceeding this amount because this causes unnecessary wear on the motor. Rotisserie motors should always be stored indoors, and, although they are generally capable of handling a little rain, they should be covered and kept dry.

For gas grills, rotisserie units need to be installed by attaching brackets to either side of the grill. Our recommendation is to try to find the specific rotisserie unit that fits your specific grill. Universal-fit rotisserie systems fit most grills, but differences in mounting locations and rotisserie rod length can be highly variable.

If a rotisserie kit is not available for your gas grill, find a universal unit with a rod that measures longer than the width of your grill. Grills are measured by the width of the cooking grates that fit inside the grill. A rotisserie rod has to stretch to inside the motor on one side and still have distance for the handle to fit on the opposite side. Rotisserie kits are sold based on the grill's width and not the total rod length.

When it comes to charcoal grills, a rotisserie system includes what is known as a riser that sits on top of the grill body and below the lid. For kettle grills, this is typically a metal ring that is 4 to 5 inches (10 to 12.7 cm) tall. Attached to this is the motor mount and a notch for the opposite end of the rod. These risers allow airflow into the charcoal grill, which makes temperature control a little more difficult.

Rotisserie units available for Kamado-style grills have a short, angled riser that lifts the grill lid about 2 inches (5 cm) and allows the rod to pass through the center of the grill. The motor mounts upside down on one end. For best results, a Kamado rotisserie unit should be used with a deflector plate for most items, though fast cooking or high-temperature rotisserie cooking may not require it.

With all units, food is secured to the rotisserie rod with a pair of forks that lock into place with thumb screws. Although some units can be tightened by hand, it is best to use a pair of pliers to ensure that the screws are held tightly in place. Do not over-tighten, but make certain that the forks are sufficiently secured so they will not move during cooking. Rotisserie cooking works by movement and as foods shift around the rod they can cause the forks to loosen. Periodically check food to see that it has not come loose. Most items will not fall off a rotisserie rod, but once loose they might not turn properly and lead to uneven cooking or burning.

Some rotisserie systems use a counterbalance to take some of the strain off of the motor. Counterbalances are metal weights near the handle. To adjust the counterbalance, first load the food item onto the rotisserie and tightly secure with the forks. Lift the rod parallel to the ground and let it roll in your hands until the heavy side naturally moves downward. Set the rod straight down so that the heavy side is at the bottom and the lift the counterbalance straight up and tighten. It is nearly impossible to get a perfectly balanced rotisserie item, but the counterbalance will reduce motor strain and increase its life span.

ROTISSERIE BASKETS

The rotisserie is perfectly designed for large roasts and whole poultry. It is not as conducive for cooking oddly shaped or smaller items. For this reason, there are rotisserie baskets that accommodate chicken pieces, smaller fish, and the like. Make sure the basket fits the grill and can rotate freely and unobstructed with the lid down before proceeding.

There are two types of rotisserie baskets: the flat basket and the tumble basket. A flat rotisserie basket is the perfect size for a pair of trout or four to six chicken leg quarters. The food items are placed in the basket and the lid locks down, holding them securely. There is usually a little play with this type of basket and it may be necessary to tie food items with kitchen twine, but as long as the food is not at risk of falling out, it is perfectly fine that it moves as the rotisserie turns.

Tumble baskets are perfect for even smaller food items, but many on the market have a little too much space between the bars to accommodate very small items. For instance, a tumble basket is a perfect solution for grilling chicken wings, but they can fall out of the basket if the wings are cut apart. Therefore, whole wings will stay in the basket, but the individual drummettes or flats may slip through. Tumble baskets are also perfect for vegetables, such as small potatoes or larger Brussels sprouts. When using a tumble basket, make sure the food item cannot get through the bars, because if it can, it will.

TOOLS FOR ROTISSERIE COOKING

Although rotisserie kits contain everything necessary for this style of cooking, there are certain tools that make the process considerably easier and safer.

Gloves: Rotisserie rods are going to get very hot on the grill. They can easily exceed 300°F to 400°F (149°C to 204°C) under some cooking conditions. At these temperatures, the rod will melt plastic cutting boards and burn skin badly. We insist on a pair of high-temperature gloves for handling rotisserie rods (as well as someone to open the door for you). There are a number of very good grilling gloves on the market, but they tend to be overpriced. What we use are welding gloves, which can be found at most any hardware store for half the price of "grilling" gloves. These gloves are not for handling food, but simply for the equipment. For getting a hold of very hot food, we recommend silicone heat-resistant food gloves, which can be found online or in any restaurant supply store. Always wear gloves when handling the rotisserie rod setup and any grilling baskets you may be using when you pull the meat off the grill.

Extension cord: Rotisserie motors come with 2 to 3 feet (61 to 91 cm) of cord, which of course is not going to reach any outlet you have. Since rotisserie motors are often operated for several hours in hot conditions, we recommend heavy-duty outdoor-rated extension cords long enough to reach your nearest (GFI) outlet, but not much longer. Extension cords can become very hot if too much amperage is drawn through them in the hot sun. Your rotisserie unit's user manual may have specific recommendations for the use of extension cords.

Thermometer: Judging the doneness of meat by touch, look, or smell is a myth. There is only one way to know the internal temperature of foods and that is with a reliable instant-read meat thermometer. For a thermometer worth having, you can spend anywhere between $20 and $100. If you are a chef, spend the $100; otherwise, buy a thermometer of reasonable quality and save a little cash.

Pliers: Even if the screws on the forks of your rotisserie unit can be easily tightened, they have a tendency to loosen on the grill. Keep a clean pair of pliers handy whenever you are loading, unloading, or adjusting your rotisserie unit. We have pliers that are kept for this purpose only so that they are clean enough to come into contact with food.

Twine: The vast majority of foods that go on the rotisserie will need tying. For this job, you will need string. Cotton kitchen twine is what works best and it can be found online or in a good restaurant supply store. It is best to have a lot of kitchen twine on hand and a little practice at this skill. There are excellent videos online that can show you how to tie any food item properly.

Sword skewer: Some rotisserie rods have a pointy end and others do not. Either way, they can be hard to guide through a beef roast, pork butt, or bone-in lamb leg. To make this process easier, a long, thin object is a must. What we use and what works best is a long sword skewer. These can be found in Middle Eastern or South Asian grocery stores and can be frequently bought individually for a ridiculously low price. Look for a skewer that is 24 inches (61 cm) long and ¼ inch (6 mm) wide and has a good handle. A sword skewer is flexible and has a sharp point, which makes it perfect for finding the path through any cut of meat to create a pilot hole for the rotisserie rod.

Drip pans: The drip pan serves many functions in rotisserie cooking. The best choice for a good drip pan is a disposable aluminum 12 x 9-inch (30.5 x 23 cm) lasagna pan that is 1 to 2 inches (2.5 to 5 cm) deep. It needs to fit the grill and food properly. Of course, with rotisserie cooking, the grates need to be removed from the grill and we recommend taking them out and getting a feel for the space.

The first thing that drip pans do is keep the grill clean and prevent flare-ups. Some meats placed on the rotisserie contain a great deal of fat, and these drippings will not only make a mess but will also catch fire—perhaps not this time, but the next time the grill is fired up. We have seen gas grills that have suffered severe damaged from grease fires after slow, indirect rotisserie cooking of a fatty cut of meat.

The second reason to use a drip pan is to add moisture to a dry cooking environment. Some of the recipes in this book favor dry roasting, while others work better with a moister cook. We will let you know with each recipe which method works best, but suffice it to say at this point that by dry, we mean an empty drip pan and by moist we mean a drip pan with water added. A water-filled drip pan will create steam that aids in cooking and helps prevent foods from drying out under the intense heat of the grill. This is important for both gas and charcoal units.

The third reason to use a drip pan is to capture drippings. If you intend to make gravy, pan sauces, or have other uses for the drippings, a clean drip pan is necessary. To prevent the drippings from drying out and burning in the drip pan, you'll need to add water. The amount of liquid needed to capture drippings is the smallest amount necessary to get to the end of the cook time without the contents all dried to a crisp. You also do not want to end up with a weak soup-filled drip pan, but once those drippings start to burn, they become useless. The necessary amount of water is not something you can always predict, so monitor the drip pan and add clean, hot water periodically for a successful gravy.

The Basics

Rotisserie cooking is easy. It may require a little patience and preparation, but done right needs little work. The basic rules are: balance well, secure tightly, use a drip pan, and watch the internal temperature. Beyond this, a rotisserie on the grill will produce vastly better food than the indoor oven every time.

Loading a Rotisserie Rod

Before you load the rotisserie rod, lift the roast with your hands, holding the cut ends. Roll it around to get a feel for the balance center. Next, because it can be hard to guide a rotisserie rod through a large piece of meat, use a long sword skewer that is is flexible and has a sharp point to create a pilot hole for the rotisserie rod. Then run the rotisserie rod through the hole and secure with the forks. Adjust the balance of the roast as necessary.

A potential problem that rotisserie cooking might pose is a loose setup. We know that we have already said several times that whatever goes on the rod must be secured tightly, but it really is the one issue that surfaces. This goes beyond pushing the forks together and tightening the screws. The food itself needs to be tied and secured into a tight package.

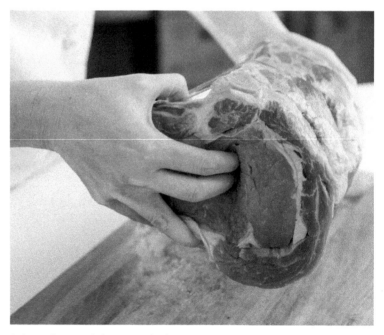

1. Locate the center balance point for the roast.

2. Make a pilot hole for the rotisserie rod.

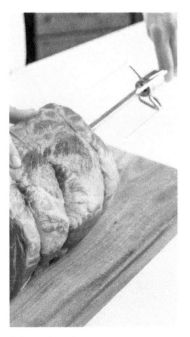

3. Insert the rod.

4. Secure the rotisserie forks.

Poultry: We could describe the process for trussing a whole bird, but it would be so much easier if you just went to the Internet and watched a one-minute video on it. Trussing is easy to do, but a little hard to describe in a book. Trussing prevents the legs and wings of poultry from flopping around and makes sure that they will stay in place. Some of the recipes we provide in this category are going to produce fall-off-the-bone chicken, and a loosely secured leg might just fall off on the grill. Not a desired outcome. Also, be sure to fold the wing tips back and under the wing to prevent them from burning or moving.

Putting a whole bird on a rotisserie skewer is easy. The rod goes in, through the neck opening and out through the body cavity. The forks are pushed together through the meat and should secure the legs to the rod. On the top, or neck end of the bird, the fork tines should slip under the breast meat and not actually pierce the breast. It is the same on the opposite side. With four-tine forks, the top tine should slide in between the two breasts. Done right, the breasts are not pieced from either side.

1. Chicken and twine for trussing.

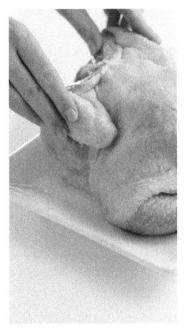

2. Fold the wings under.

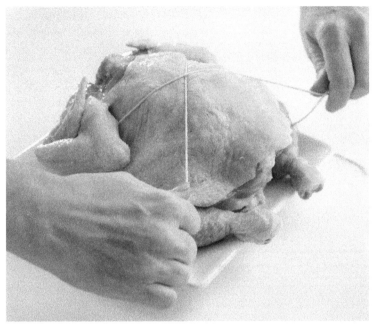

3. Secure the wings.

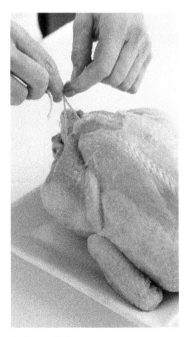

4. Secure the legs.

5. Tie the legs.

Boneless roasts: The perfect item for the rotisserie is shaped like a cylinder. Unfortunately, most roasts are not shaped that way. Take, for instance, one of our favorite beef roasts for the rotisserie, the chuck. This is a flat, rectangular-shaped piece of beef that is loose and will move around too much on the rod if not tied properly. While you can ask your butcher to tie it for you, it is an easy process to turn this hunk of meat into a respectable roast.

To tie a roast like this, lay it flat on a large cutting board. Trim off any loose pieces or unwanted fat, and then take a long piece of kitchen string and center it under the roast. Bring up the ends around the roast and tie with a simple knot. Pull very tightly, bringing the roast together. Switch the strings in your hands in a circular pattern three times. This will secure the knot so it will not slip before you add another knot. Now, moving out from the center, do this two more times on each side of the first string at equal distances. You should now have a tight roast that is ready to be skewered and placed on the rotisserie rod.

To get this roast onto the rod, run your sword skewer lengthwise through the center of the roast and out the other side. You now have the pilot hole for the rotisserie rod. Before you do anything else, and believe me we have forgotten this before, place one of the forks onto the rotisserie rod, letting it sit near the handle with the tines pointing toward the roast. Center the meat and push the forks together as tightly as possible. Secure the screws and it is ready for the preheated grill.

1. Roast and twine.

2. Tie a knot in the center of the roast.

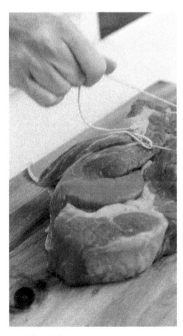

3. Pull tightly to secure.

4. Clip the loose ends of twine.

1. Tenderloins and twine.

2. Stack the tenderloins and tie them end to end.

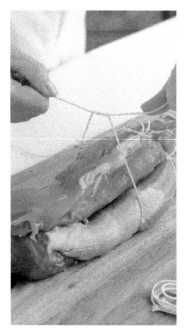

3. Tie the twine every two inches (5 cm).

4. Cut off the excess twine.

1. Remove the bone from the lamb leg.

2. Butterfly the lamb leg into uniform thickness.

1. Layer the roast with bacon and tie at the end.

2. Tie every two inches (5 cm) to secure the bacon.

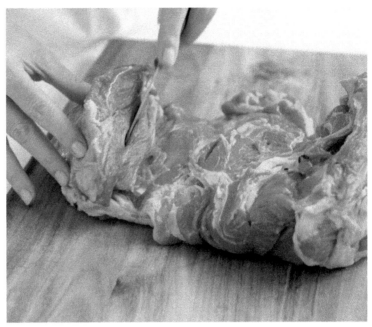

1. The first cut should be an inch or two (2.5 to 5 cm) from the end of the roast.

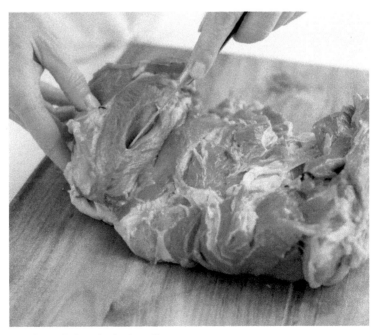

2. Make small, deep slits for the stuffing.

Bone-in roasts and leg of lamb: These can be a more of a challenge. This is where the sword skewer really comes in handy. To secure a piece of meat like this to the rotisserie rod you need to find the balance center and then find a path through the meat as close as possible to that line. In general, most cuts work out perfectly fine. Some roasts might present a bit of a challenge, but with a little patience it is not that difficult. A bone-in leg of lamb has more meat on one side of the bone than the other, and the rotisserie rod should run right along the bone to find the perfect center. In all our years of rotisserie cooking we have yet to find a piece of meat we could not get onto a rotisserie rod.

Preparing the Grill

Before the spit can be set, the grill needs to be prepared. The first step is to make sure that the rotisserie system is installed according to the manufacturer's instructions, has access to power, and turns properly. This should be tested before food is put on the rod to ensure that everything is working correctly. Make certain the rotisserie rod will turn with the grill lid closed. All of the recipes in this book require the lid to be down for the food to properly roast.

The cooking grates will need to be removed from the grill to allow space for foods to turn. The tents that sit over the burners of the gas grill should be left in place to protect the burners from drippings. Preheat the grill before placing food on it. This is particularly important with charcoal grilling, as adding charcoal to the grill will create a cloud of ash. If your charcoal grill needs refueling, light the charcoal separately in a charcoal chimney and remove the rotisserie rod and food from the grill before pouring in the burning coals. Allow the ashes to settle before putting the food back on the grill.

Once the food is on the grill, make sure that the rotisserie unit is turning. It may be necessary to adjust the counterbalance (if your unit has one). Carefully close the lid, watching to make sure that the food item does not come into contact with the lid or any other part of the grill. With whole poultry, check to see that the trussing remains intact and the legs and wings don't come loose and hang. This will cause these parts to burn quickly.

As food cooks, it will shrink. Roasts will generally shrink the most. As these large items cook, it may be necessary to tighten the rotisserie forks. To do this, stop the rotisserie and, with heatproof gloves and a pair of pliers, loosen the nut holding one of the forks in place and push it toward the other fork. Retighten the nut and resume cooking. If this needs to be done more than once, which is rare, take turns with the forks to keep the food as centered in the grill as possible.

Once everything is loaded, secured, and turning freely, it is time to let it go. Our recipes give a general guide to how long it will take each item to cook. These times should be looked at as a guide only. Depending on the type of grill used, weather conditions, and variations in cuts of meat, these times will vary. Long before we say something should be done it will be time to start checking the temperature. Of course, anything on the grill needs to be monitored, so never leave a rotisserie item unattended for very long.

The rule when testing for temperature with anything on the rotisserie is to push the probe of an instant-read thermometer into the deepest part of the meat, but well away from the rotisserie rod. The rod will conduct heat through a food item, roasts in particular, and cause that area to cook faster. Look for a test location that is in the thickest part of the meat, an equal distance between the rod and the outside surface. Test several locations before deciding that something is completely done and test both ends, since the grill might not cook food evenly.

With poultry, test each of the breasts in the very center and each thigh in the thickest part. It is always better to check several times than to be unsure whether the meat, especially poultry, is properly cooked. Ideal temperatures for doneness are provided with each recipe.

We always recommend removing roasts (beef, lamb, and pork) from the grill before they are up to the perfect temperature and then allow them to rest. Resting meats before carving allows juices to flow back into place and helps prevent foods from drying out. During this resting phase, the center portion of large cuts of meat will continue to cook and the internal temperature will rise. Remove these items 5°F (2°C) below the ideal temperature, place on a warm platter or cutting board, cover with aluminum foil, and allow the meat to rest for 10 to 15 minutes. Then and only then is the meat ready to carve.

Drip Pan Cooking

There is a pan, there is heat, why not cook something? From our experience, there is not a hearty vegetable that cannot be cooked this way. Add some chopped potatoes, beets, winter or summer squash, or mushrooms to the pan. Season lightly and let the drippings do the rest. We do recommend that drip pan vegetables are cooked under fattier beef roasts, like rib roasts or chuck roasts, and rotisserie chickens. Remember to keep the flavor profile in mind and try to pair vegetables with simply seasoned meats.

In most cases, the cook time for a drip pan dish is less that the item spinning on the rotisserie above it. This means that the drip pan item needs to be added after the food above it has already spent some time cooking. There are two ways to go about this and the difference has to do with how much fat is going to be dripping from the food above. If there is a lot of fat, it is best to remove the drip pan that you have been using, along with the drippings, and add a new pan already filled with food. If the rotisserie item does not produce a lot of drippings, then you can add the drip pan items to the pan at the recommended time.

One thing to watch for is flooding. This is particularly problematic with rib roasts because they contain so much fat and the drippings collected in the pan can be excessive. No one wants a grease-filled pan of potatoes. If this should happen, simply drain off the excess fat into a separate container or use a turkey baster to remove the drippings. Return the food to the grill and cook until done. Use your judgment and always taste foods prepared this way before serving; adjust the seasoning accordingly.

Testing for Doneness

When cooking food on the rotisserie, there are two scenarios. With a typical gas grill, without a rotisserie burner, the heat is going to come at the food from the ends. This means that the ends will cook faster than the middle. It is also why it is very important that the food item be centered between the burners. When testing for doneness with a reliable instant-read thermometer, test in the center of the roast and in the middle space between the rotisserie rod and the outside surface of the food. Rotisserie rods get hot and will actually cook the center of roasts more quickly. This is why rotisserie cooking is a faster method of cooking than simple roasting.

With a charcoal grill or rotisserie burner, the heat approaches the food much more evenly. While centering the food is not as important, the fire should reach it as equally as possible. Test for doneness in several locations along the food item, in a space away from the rotisserie rod.

When testing poultry for doneness, test in several locations, including the center of the breast and in the joint location where the leg attaches to the body. This is the slowest cooking location and must be above 165°F (74°C) to be safe and should be at least 175°F (80°C) to be palatable.

When testing for doneness with an instant-read thermometer, test in the center of the roast and in the middle space between the rod and the surface of the food.

CHAPTER 1

BRINES, RUBS, MARINADES, AND BASTES

Before anything goes on the rotisserie, the flavors need to be considered. Proper seasoning starts before the cooking and there are many options available to make the most of whatever turns on the spit. Because of the high, dry heat, a good place to start is with a brine. Although brines don't add a great deal of savory flavors, they put moisture and the proper amount of salt directly into the meat. This is a particularly good place to start with poultry and pork, because brines keep these lean meats moist and tender.

Brines, of course, take a few hours to work, so a quicker and easier way to add flavor is with a spice rub. The seasoning blends you make yourself are packed with flavor. Since all of these rotisserie items tend to be large, rubs should be applied in healthy doses to make the most of their power. As the meats cook, rubs blend with the natural juices and help form the crusty surfaces that make these dishes stand out.

Marinades take the rub to a liquid form and lather on flavors as well as create a protective barrier on meats, allowing them to take the intense heat of the grill better. Marinades are always a great choice and should be applied a few hours before cooking starts. Our recipes that call for marinades will tell you how long to marinate the meat, but one thing is for sure: To get maximum flavor, marinades are generally the way to go.

Bastes are applied to foods as they cook. This can be done once or several times. A good baste adds moisture and flavor in thin, even layers while the rotisserie items turn. In general, bastes should be applied up to the last 30 minutes of cooking so that they have time to roast in place.

We have carefully selected the best strategy for flavoring the recipes in this book. However, feel free to experiment, not only with each of these methods but also with the combinations. Bastes work perfectly with any of these methods—in fact, we frequently include rubs with our bastes—and use marinades (reserve a portion, of course; do not use what the meat was soaking in) as bastes.

BRINES

A brine is a magical solution that is guaranteed to improve practically every large piece of meat that gets put on a rotisserie rod. A brine is also a simple way to make something spectacular. Some cuts of meat, though lean and flavorful, need help retaining moisture. Brining is the best way to make a good cut of meat better. Pork and poultry in particular benefit from a good brining.

The method is straightforward. A brine is simply a saltwater solution that meats are soaked in for an allotted amount of time. There must be enough brine to completely cover the meat or poultry and enough time for it to work. For a whole chicken, the brining time is 6 to 8 hours, though times up to 12 hours are perfectly fine. A pork tenderloin should brine for 2 to 4 hours, while a large pork loin roast should get 8 to 10 hours. A whole turkey should brine for 24 hours.

A proper brine is 1 part salt, 1 part sugar to balance the flavor, and 16 parts water. Combine vigorously to ensure that the salt and sugar are completely dissolved. Place the brine and the meat in a container (not metal because it can react with the salt) and refrigerate for 30 minutes to an hour. For small amounts of meat, a good-quality resealable plastic bag works well for brining, but any plastic or glass bowl, covered, will also work.

If a meat has been brined it will contain all the salt it needs for flavor. *When brining, omit salt from rubs and bastes for the rest of the recipe*, or the salt content may be too high to be palatable. Do not worry too much about the specifics here. In the recipes where we recommend using a brine, we provide the exact amounts and times.

1. The basic brine ingredients: water, salt, and sugar.

2. Spices can also be added to the brine.

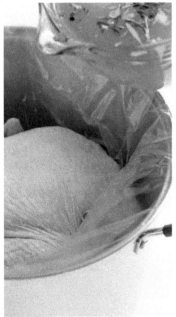

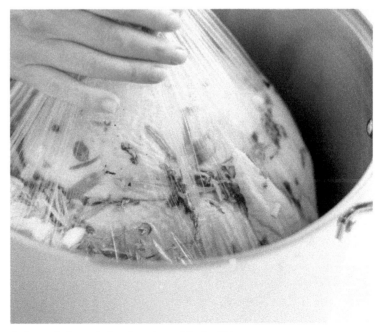

3. Place the turkey in a large plastic bag and cover with brine.

4. Secure the bag and allow the turkey to brine for 24 hours.

Basic Brine

¼ cup (72 g) table salt or
⅓ cup (95 g) kosher salt

¼ cup (50 g) sugar

1 quart (1 L) cold water

Yield: 1 quart (1 L)

This is the basic recipe or formula for making a brining solution. It has the proper proportion of salt and sugar to water to balance the flavors. Depending on what is being brined and the container used to hold both the meat and brine, the recipe may need to be adjusted. It is best to have too much brine than not enough and the total volume of brine should be double that of what is being brined. For example, a whole chicken will require that this recipe be doubled.

Combine all the ingredients in a large glass or plastic container and stir until the salt and sugar are completely dissolved. Keeping the solution as cold as possible, place it in a large, nonmetal container. Add the food being brined and make sure it is completely submerged. Refrigerate for the total brining time.

Pork Brine

⅔ cup (132 g) sugar

¾ cup (216 g) kosher salt

1½ gallons (5.4 L)
ice cold water

⅓ cup (107 g) honey

4 to 6 bay leaves

6 sprigs fresh thyme

2 tablespoons (2.6 g)
dried parsley

1½ teaspoons peppercorns

Yield: 1½ gallons (5.4 L)

Brines, of course, can do more than just the magic of adding moisture and tenderness. They can carry flavor into meats. By adding spices, herbs, and other aromatics, a brine can make meat more flavorful. This brine goes perfectly with pork.

In a large glass or plastic container, dissolve the sugar and salt in the water by stirring until the water turns clear. Add the remaining ingredients and stir thoroughly. Submerge the pork, cover, and place in the refrigerator. Brine the pork for 4 to 12 hours, depending on the size of the cut.

Spiced Poultry Brine

1 gallon (3.7 L) ice cold water

1½ cups (432 g) kosher salt

½ cup (120 ml) white vinegar

⅓ cup (75 g) packed
brown sugar

4 cloves garlic, smashed

4 bay leaves

1 tablespoon (6 g)
pickling spice

1 teaspoon ground allspice

1 teaspoon freshly
ground black pepper

1 teaspoon dried tarragon

Yield: 1 gallon (3.7 L)

Use this brine for any kind of poultry, including turkey, chicken, and even Cornish game hens. Halve the recipe for smaller items.

In a large glass or plastic container, stir together all the ingredients until the salt and sugar have dissolved. Submerge the poultry completely in the brine, cover, and store in the refrigerator or a large ice-packed cooler. Brine turkey for 24 hours, chicken for 4 hours, and Cornish game hens for 2 hours.

HOLIDAY BRINE

1 gallon (3.7 L) ice cold water

1¼ cups (360 g) kosher salt

½ cup (112 g) packed
brown sugar

1 gallon (3.7 L) vegetable
or chicken stock

2½ tablespoons (15 g)
candied ginger

1¼ tablespoons (7.5 g)
allspice berries

1¼ tablespoons (6 g)
peppercorns

6 bay leaves

Yield: 2 gallons (7.5 L)

*This brine is perfect for holiday turkeys and pork roasts.
The recipe makes enough solution for a 15- to 20-pound
(6.8 to 9 kg) turkey. It can be scaled as needed for a wide
range of meats.*

Stir all the ingredients together in a large glass or plastic bowl or food-safe bucket until the salt and sugar have dissolved completely. Submerge the turkey in the brine, cover, and refrigerate for 24 hours. Brine pork roasts for 8 to 12 hours.

RUBS

In the traditional barbecue world, a rub is a combination of salt, sweet, color, and flavor. It serves not only to season meat but also helps create a crusty surface and provides texture. We use rubs throughout this book, but here we include a few fantastic all-purpose recipes. The proportions are designed for a single use, but these can be made in large batches and stored for up to 6 months in a cool and dark place. The advantage of using a rub is that it is easier to apply in an even coating than adding all the seasonings individually. By putting the herbs, spices, and other ingredients together first, it creates an even distribution of flavor. The rule with rubs is what sticks is the amount needed and you do not actually have to do any rubbing. Sprinkle on in even layers and what stays on the meat is the perfect proportion.

Beef Roast and Steak Rub

¼ cup (72 g) kosher salt

2 tablespoons (12 g) coarsely ground black pepper

2 tablespoons (7 g) onion powder

2 teaspoons garlic powder

2 teaspoons dried marjoram

Yield: A little more than ½ cup (95 g)

What a good, simple beef rub does is accentuate its natural flavor. While this is the perfect rub for all cuts and quality of rotisserie beef, it might just be a good idea to make up a large batch to keep on hand for grilling steaks as well.

Mix all the ingredients in a small bowl. Apply evenly to the meat and cook as directed. This rub can be prepared ahead of time and stored in an airtight container in a cool, dark place for up to 6 months.

Basic Barbecue Pork Rub

½ cup (112 g) packed brown sugar

¼ cup (28 g) paprika

1½ tablespoons (27 g) kosher salt

2 teaspoons mustard powder

1 teaspoon cayenne

½ teaspoon garlic powder

Yield: Scant 1 cup (180 g)

This is one of our favorite go-to rub recipes for barbecued pork, and by barbecued pork we mean any cut of pork that is looking for a touch of barbecue flavor, regardless of how it is cooked. About half this recipe is enough for the average pork roast, but you might want to double the recipe and keep it on hand. It is also the perfect rub for grilled pork chops.

Combine all the ingredients in a small bowl and apply all over pork roast. This rub can be prepared ahead of time and stored in an airtight container in a cool, dark place for up to 6 months.

Basic Poultry Rub

1 tablespoon (18 g) salt

1 tablespoon (9 g) dry mustard

2 teaspoons sugar

1 teaspoon sweet paprika

1 teaspoon celery salt

½ teaspoon ground
black pepper

¼ teaspoon ground allspice

¼ teaspoon garlic powder

Yield: ¼ cup (30 g)

This is a fantastic rub for chicken. However, you can use this on turkey or Cornish game hens as well. Adjust the recipe to suit your needs. Obviously, you will need a little less for a smaller bird and more for a whole turkey.

Mix all the ingredients in a small bowl and apply evenly to the poultry. This rub can be prepared ahead of time and stored in an airtight container in a cool, dark place for up to 6 months.

MARINADES

For reasons that make little sense, marinades have become something of a controversial subject. Long ago, the myth that marinades could turn a tough roast into tender goodness was rabidly debunked by people who did not seem to understand the real advantage of a marinade. A good marinade is an equal combination of oil and vinegar plus herbs and seasonings. The purpose of a marinade is to add oil and flavor to the surface of foods that are cooked at a high temperature. The oil acts as a protective barrier that helps hold in moisture and allows the surface to cook a little slower without drying out too quickly. A marinade is not a miracle cure for a bad cut of meat, but it goes a long way to making a tough or dry cut better. If you do not believe us, try our recipe for Chipotle Barbacoa Chuck Roast (page 88). It is one of our favorites, and it is the marinade that makes it fantastic.

Classic Beef Marinade

⅓ cup (80 ml)
red wine vinegar

¼ cup (60 ml) vegetable
or olive oil

2 cloves garlic, minced

2 teaspoons salt

1 teaspoon freshly
ground black pepper

1 teaspoon onion powder

¼ teaspoon dried thyme

*Yield: A little more than
½ cup (140 ml)*

This marinade can be used on any type of beef roast or steak. You can double the recipe as needed. We recommend this for tougher cuts like sirloin, eye of round, or flat steaks.

1. Combine all the ingredients in a large bowl. Use immediately or store in an airtight container in the refrigerator for up to 1 week.

2. Marinate steaks for 6 hours, roasts for 12 to 24 hours.

PORK MARINADE

½ cup (120 ml) apple juice

¼ cup (60 ml)
apple cider vinegar

2 tablespoons (30 ml) olive oil

2 tablespoons (30 ml)
maple syrup

2 cloves garlic, smashed

1 teaspoon salt

½ teaspoon paprika

1 or 2 large, fresh sage
leaves, chopped

Yield: 1 cup (235 ml)

This is a basic marinade for all pork cuts. As stated before, double or triple the recipe based on the size of the roast. Clearly, you won't need as much marinade for a pork tenderloin as you would for a pork butt, shoulder, or leg. The cider vinegar, sage, and maple syrup add a nice hint of autumn to any pork dish you prepare.

1. Combine all the marinade ingredients in a medium-size bowl. Let stand at room temperature for 30 minutes. Use immediately or store in the refrigerator for up to 1 week.

2. Marinate tenderloin for 4 hours and larger cuts for 12 to 24 hours.

Chicken Marinade

¼ cup (60 ml) white vinegar

¼ cup (60 ml) balsamic vinegar

½ cup (120 ml) olive oil

2 cloves garlic, minced

2 teaspoons salt

1¼ teaspoons freshly ground black pepper

1 teaspoon dried oregano

½ teaspoon dried marjoram

Yield: About 1 cup (240 ml)

Yes, we are aware that this is titled chicken marinade, but this marinade can be used on turkey as well. Just double the amount called for in the recipe. This is a particularly good recipe if you decide to forgo brining your poultry of choice. The acids and salt will help keep your chicken or turkey from drying out on the grill and will instead render a tender, juicy bird.

1. Place the white vinegar and balsamic in a bowl and slowly whisk in the oil. Add the remaining ingredients. Use immediately or store in the refrigerator for up to 1 week.

2. Marinate whole chickens for 6 to 12 hours, chicken leg quarters for 4 hours. Double or triple the recipe for large poultry. Marinate turkeys for 12 to 24 hours.

BASTES

Rotisserie cooking is, as we have said, inherently self-basting. This means that one of the best ways to enhance the flavor of meats and vegetables that go on the spit is by using a baste. Why not add extra flavor to your meal while it is cooking? A baste should be thin and packed with flavor. The object is to paint it into place and allow the turning of the rotisserie to keep it rotating. As food cooks, the moisture evaporates, leaving behind all the concentrated flavors.

There are two things about basting that need to be mentioned. First, a baste will cool the surface of meat, slowing the cooking process. This is not a bad thing. It can actually buy you time by slowing the process and it can help keep that slow roasting, well, slow. Warm bastes before you apply them, but do not apply hot. The perfect temperature for a baste at the time of application is between 120°F and 140°F (49°C and 60°C). This is warm enough not to dramatically cool the food, but cool enough not to cook the surface.

The second point about bastes is the sugar content. Some bastes, including ones we use in this book, contain sugar. Sugar will start to burn around 265°F (130°C). This means that bastes that contain sugar need to be applied toward the end of the cooking time. Adding them too early can produce a burnt flavor.

One option for a baste is actually barbecue sauce. It can be thick or thin and generally contains sugar, so it is applied only toward the end of the cooking time. Barbecue sauce should be cooked onto food and not simply poured over the top after the meat has been removed from the grill.

Easy Barbecue Sauce

1 tablespoon (15 ml) vegetable oil

2 cloves garlic, minced

1¾ cups (420 g) ketchup

¼ cup (60 ml) apple cider vinegar

¼ cup (60 ml) water

¼ cup (60 g) packed brown sugar

1 tablespoon (14 g) unsalted butter (do not use margarine)

2 teaspoons Worcestershire sauce

¼ teaspoon cayenne

¼ teaspoon salt

¼ teaspoon ground black pepper

Yield: 2½ cups (600 g)

This recipe is a simple tomato-based barbecue sauce that can be made on your stove top. We recommend that you use this on just about any cut of pork or chicken. Just make sure that the seasoning rub is quite neutral and will actually go with a sauce like this. Although this recipe does not call for liquid smoke, you can add a teaspoon or two to the sauce to create some smokiness.

1. Heat the vegetable oil in a medium-size saucepan over medium heat. Add the minced garlic and cook for 30 seconds, until it becomes fragrant. Do not let the garlic burn or brown. This will cause it to become bitter and will ruin the sauce. Add the ketchup, vinegar, water, and brown sugar. Simmer over medium heat for 3 to 4 minutes, stirring often. Add the remaining ingredients, decrease the heat to low, and simmer for 5 more minutes.

2. Remove the sauce from the heat and let cool for 10 minutes before using as a baste. If making ahead of time, allow the sauce to cool for 30 minutes and place in an airtight container. Store in the refrigerator for up to 10 days. Reheat before using.

Smoky Baste

1½ cups (355 ml) apple cider vinegar

⅓ cup (80 ml) water

Juice of 1 lemon

2 tablespoons (30 ml) Worcestershire sauce

1½ teaspoons smoked paprika

1 teaspoon liquid smoke (use more if desired)

Yield: About 2 cups (470 ml)

This is a great baste for large cuts of pork or turkey. It offers a little extra smoky flavor for meats on the rotisserie. Use with or without the addition of a smoke packet to simulate low and slow barbecue.

1. Combine all the ingredients in a bowl and let sit for 15 minutes before using.

2. Baste onto rotisserie meats halfway through the cooking time. Double the recipe for larger items like a turkey or pork leg.

LEMON-HERB BASTE

1 cup (235 ml) dry white wine

Zest and juice of 1 lemon

¼ cup (60 ml) water

2 bay leaves

2 teaspoons chopped
fresh rosemary

1 teaspoon chopped
fresh thyme

1 teaspoon lemon pepper

½ teaspoon garlic powder

¼ teaspoon salt
(omit if brining the meat)

¼ teaspoon ground
black pepper

Yield: About 1⅓ cups (305 ml)

This simple herb and wine baste works well with pork, poultry, some cuts of beef, and fish. The trick is to remember to use this baste with like flavors.

1. Combine all the ingredients in a bowl and let sit for 15 to 30 minutes before using.

2. Baste onto meats halfway through the cooking time. The baste can be made a day ahead of time, but it must be brought up to room temperature before using.

Beurre Blanc

¼ cup (40 g) finely
chopped onion

¼ cup (60 ml) dry white wine

¼ cup (60 ml)
white wine vinegar

2 cups (4 sticks, 450 g)
unsalted butter, cut into cubes

½ teaspoon chopped
fresh thyme

Yield: 4 servings

This is a traditional French butter and wine sauce that is served on top of chicken and fish.

1. In a saucepan, bring the chopped onion, white wine, and vinegar to a simmer on the stove top. Cook until the mixture is reduced by half, stirring often. This process will take about 6 minutes or so.

2. Lower the heat to medium-low and begin adding the butter a few cubes at a time. When one set has melted, add a bit more and continue until all the butter has been added.

3. Continue cooking until the sauce has thickened nicely, then add the chopped thyme, stir a few times, and remove from the heat. Serve immediately.

4. If making ahead of time, store in a sealed container in the refrigerator, then reheat and serve.

A baste should be thin and packed with flavor. The object is to paint it into place and allow the turning of the rotisserie to keep it rotating.

CHAPTER 2

BEEF

Beef is, of course, a favorite meat in much of the world as well as in the United States. It's versatile, hearty, and . . . well, beefy. It is also the most popular meat to hit a grill, typically in the form of steaks and burgers. Surprisingly, large beef roasts are not as popular, unless it is a big, fatty brisket being loaded into a smoker to make Texas's preferred barbecue.

In general, all those beef roasts in the meat counter at the grocery store end up in a countertop slow cooker or braised in the oven. Dry roasting seems reserved for rib roasts and then only for very special occasions.

We like beef. We like roast beef and we like it on the grill, where it can develop a variety of textures. Braised beef is slow-boiled beef and, while delicious, the meat gives up much of its natural flavors to the braising liquid. This is not so with rotisserie beef.

Our favorite cuts of beef for the rotisserie are tri-tip and chuck roasts (though we have recipes here for almost every type of beef roast). These two roasts have the fat content and marbling that keep them tender and juicy on the grill. They also have the virtue of being less expensive than most beef roasts.

Most roasts must be tied into a shape suitable for the rotisserie. You can ask your butcher to do this or simply do it yourself. It requires some string and about five minutes of handiwork. It's not that difficult and it's a great skill to have.

Our all-time favorite beef roast is the king of roasts, the prime rib. It's loaded with flavor, incredibly tender meat, and the kind of fat that bastes the beef to perfection. Although the bones add weight to the roast (remember the maximum capacity of your rotisserie motor), we always cook a bone-in rib roast. A great trick for bone-in prime rib is to cut off the bones (or have the butcher do it), season the roast all the way around, and then tie the bones back in place. It takes a few extra minutes, but it adds a lot of flavor. The surprising thing about the bones on a prime rib is that no matter how many we cook, the bones never seem to make it to the table.

Santa Maria Tri-Tip Roast

Rub

1½ tablespoons (27 g) kosher salt

2 teaspoons freshly ground black pepper

1½ teaspoons sugar

1 teaspoon garlic powder

½ teaspoon ancho chile powder or 1 teaspoon chili powder

2 tri-tip roasts, 2 pounds (908 g) each

Baste

⅓ cup (80 ml) water

1 tablespoon (14 g) rub mixture

1 tablespoon (15 ml) white vinegar

Yield: 8 servings

Down in Santa Maria, California, tri-tip means barbecue. This traditional dish goes back about two hundred years and was a favorite of the cowboys who worked the region. Once unknown outside of California, tri-tip is a cut of beef that has grown in popularity and is now widely available around the world. To keep with the California tradition, serve this with pinquito beans and a tossed green salad. This recipe is best done over charcoal, as it has been for years. If you like an extra saucy tri-tip, double the sauce recipe and reserve half to serve with the roast.

1. Prepare the grill for medium-high heat with indirect cooking.

2. To make the rub: Combine the rub ingredients in a small bowl. Reserve 1 tablespoon (14 g) of the mixture for the baste. Apply the remaining rub on both sides of the tri-tip roasts. Let sit for 10 to 15 minutes before threading onto the rotisserie rod.

3. To make the baste: Combine the baste ingredients in a small bowl, mix well, and set aside.

4. Place one tri-tip on top of the other with the small ends on opposite sides. Fold in these ends and tie the roasts with kitchen twine, creating one single, uniform roast. Run a long sword skewer through the center of the roast lengthwise to create a pilot hole. Run the rotisserie rod through the hole and secure with the forks. Balance as necessary.

5. Place the roast on the preheated grill, set a drip pan underneath, and add 1 to 2 cups (235 to 470 ml) hot water to the pan. Cook the roast for 80 to 90 minutes. During the last 30 minutes of cooking time, begin basting with the sauce. Do this 6 to 8 times, until the roast is well coated and the internal temperature is near 140°F (60°C). The roast will shrink during the cooking process, so adjust the forks when appropriate.

6. Carefully remove the rotisserie forks and slide the rod out, and then place the roast on a large cutting board. Cover the meat with aluminum foil and let rest for 15 minutes. Cut off the twine. Separate the roasts, slice against the grain, and serve.

Dr Pepper Tri-Tip Roast

2 tri-tip roasts,
2 pounds (908 g) each

Sauce

¾ cup (180 g) ketchup

¾ cup (180 ml) Dr Pepper

¼ cup (60 g) packed
brown sugar

2 teaspoons apple
cider vinegar

¼ teaspoon freshly
ground black pepper

⅛ teaspoon salt

Rub

1 tablespoon (18 g) kosher salt

1½ teaspoons freshly
ground black pepper

1½ teaspoons paprika

1½ teaspoons mild
chili powder

½ teaspoon garlic powder

Yield: 8 servings

There is a long-standing tradition of using cola in barbecue sauces, particularly Dr Pepper. It has the right amount of sweetness to balance the sauce, while adding a bit of uniqueness that is typical of this type of cola. The other component, the tri-tip roast, is the meat of choice for the Santa Maria barbecue tradition. So, this recipe is a fusion of California and Southern cooking and more than excellent enough to justify using two tri-tip roasts. If you like an extra saucy tri-tip, double the sauce recipe and reserve half to serve with the roast.

1. Prepare the grill for medium-high heat with indirect cooking.

2. Place one tri-tip on top of the other with the small ends on opposite sides. Fold in these ends and tie the roasts with kitchen twine, creating one single, uniform roast. Run a long sword skewer through the center of the roast lengthwise to create a pilot hole. Run the rotisserie rod through the hole and secure with the forks. Balance as necessary.

3. To make the sauce: Combine the sauce ingredients in a small saucepan and simmer over medium heat for 5 to 6 minutes, stirring often. Watch for burning and lower the heat if necessary. Remove from the heat and let sit for 15 to 30 minutes before using.

4. To make the rub: Combine the rub ingredients in a small bowl and evenly apply all over the roast.

5. Place the roast on the preheated grill, set a drip pan underneath, and add 1 to 2 cups (235 to 470 ml) hot water to the pan. Cook the roast for 80 to 90 minutes. During the last 30 minutes of cooking time, begin basting with the sauce. Do this 6 to 8 times, until the roast is well coated with the barbecue sauce and the internal temperature reaches 140°F (60°C). The roast will shrink during the cooking process, so adjust the forks when appropriate.

6. Remove the roast from the grill, carefully remove the rotisserie forks and slide the rod out, and then place the roast on a large cutting board. Cover the meat with aluminum foil and let rest for 12 to 15 minutes. Cut off the twine. Separate the roasts, slice against the grain, and serve.

Argentine Tri-Tip with Chimichurri Sauce

Chimichurri Sauce

½ cup (30 g) packed fresh flat-leaf parsley, chopped

⅓ cup (6 g) packed fresh cilantro leaves, chopped

3 or 4 cloves garlic

1 small shallot, chopped

2 tablespoons (30 ml) white vinegar

¼ teaspoon salt

¼ teaspoon freshly ground black pepper

¼ teaspoon red pepper flakes (optional)

½ cup (120 ml) olive oil

2 tri-tip roasts, 4 to 5 pounds (1.8 to 2.3 kg) each

Rub

1½ tablespoons (27 g) kosher salt

2 teaspoons freshly ground black pepper

1 teaspoon onion powder

½ teaspoon cayenne

Yield: 10 to 12 servings

This is a simple Argentine-style tri-tip recipe to try on the rotisserie. It is normally placed on the grill, but the rotisserie provides a self-basting action that results in a far more tender tri-tip. Because this roast has a nearly triangular shape, it is best to cook two at a time. By overlaying the two roasts and tying them together, it forms a perfectly balanced uniform roast.

1. To make the chimichurri sauce: Prepare the sauce 1 to 2 hours before the meat will be finished cooking. Place all the sauce ingredients, except the oil, into a food processor. Pulse a few times. Slowly pour in the oil while pulsing 10 or so more times. You do not want to purée the chimichurri, but all the ingredients should be finely chopped and well combined with the oil. Remove the sauce from the food processor, transfer to a bowl, and set aside until ready to eat.

2. Prepare the grill for medium-high heat with indirect cooking.

3. Place one tri-tip on top of the other with the small ends on opposite sides. Fold in these ends and tie the roasts with kitchen twine, creating one single, uniform roast. Run a long sword skewer through the center of the roast lengthwise to create a pilot hole. Run the rotisserie rod through the hole and secure with the forks. Balance as necessary.

4. To make the rub: Combine the rub ingredients in a small bowl and apply evenly all over the meat.

5. Place the roast on the preheated grill and set a drip pan underneath. Cook the roast for 70 to 90 minutes, or until near the desired doneness. The roast will shrink during the cooking process, so adjust the forks when appropriate.

6. Carefully remove the rotisserie forks and slide the rod out, and then place the roast on a large cutting board. Cover the meat with aluminum foil and let rest for 15 minutes. Cut off the twine. Separate the roasts, slice against the grain ⅓ to ½ inch (8 to 13 mm) thick and serve with the chimichurri sauce.

BEEF BRISKET

1 untrimmed brisket flat, 6 to 7 pounds (2.7 to 3.2 kg)

Marinade

⅓ cup (80 ml) olive oil

½ cup (120 ml) red wine vinegar

Juice of 1 large lemon

2 cloves garlic, smashed

1 tablespoon (11 g) yellow mustard

2 teaspoons Worcestershire sauce

½ teaspoon salt

Rub

⅓ cup (75 g) packed brown sugar

2½ tablespoons (45 g) kosher salt

2 tablespoons (14 g) paprika

2 tablespoons (14 g) mild chili powder

1 tablespoon (6 g) freshly ground black pepper

2 teaspoons onion powder

Yield: 8 servings

This is not your average barbecued beef brisket cooked low and slow on the grill. The rotisserie method renders a completely different finished product. Although the brisket is seasoned the same, the texture will be a bit different. We recommend slicing these brisket "rolls" very thinly and using it in sandwiches. It will be absolutely delicious.

1. The brisket flat will generally be uneven. Using a sharp knife, trim the brisket into a uniform and equally thick rectangle, leaving a layer of fat on one side about ¼ inch (6 mm) thick. Save any trimmings for soup and stews, or grind for burgers. Cut into 3 equal-size sections.

2. To make the marinade: Combine the marinade ingredients in a bowl.

3. Place the brisket thirds into a large resealable plastic bag. Pour in the marinade, seal, and, in light squeezing motions, work the marinade all over the meat. Place in the refrigerator and marinate for 12 to 24 hours.

4. Prepare the grill for medium heat with indirect cooking. This recipe works best on charcoal but can be done on a gas grill, though the smoke quality won't be as good.

5. Remove the meat from the marinade and place on a large cutting board. Roll each brisket into a "C" shape with the fat on the outside. Run a long sword skewer through each piece in two places toward the ends to create pilot holes. Thread the brisket pieces onto the rotisserie rod through each hole and secure tightly. Tie if necessary to hold the roasts in place. These pieces will shrink as they cook and the centerpiece may stop turning. It may be necessary to retighten everything during cooking.

6. To make the rub: Combine the rub ingredients in a small bowl. Apply liberally to the brisket pieces. Let sit for 10 minutes.

7. Place the brisket on the grill with a drip pan underneath. Cook for 5 to 6 hours over medium-low heat, until the brisket is near an internal temperature of 185°F (85°C) to 190°F (88°C).

8. Carefully remove the rotisserie forks and slide the rod out, and then wrap tightly with aluminum foil. Let the meat rest for 30 minutes before slicing.

Garlic-Herb Prime Rib Roast

One 4-bone prime rib roast
(8 to 10 pounds, or
3.6 to 4.5 kg)

Rub

¼ cup (72 g) coarse kosher
or sea salt

8 cloves garlic, minced

2 tablespoons (30 ml) olive oil

2 tablespoons (6 g)
chopped fresh marjoram

1 tablespoon (6 g) coarsely
ground black pepper

2 teaspoons orange zest

2 teaspoons chopped
fresh thyme

Yield: 8 to 10 servings

This is the perfect French-inspired, garlic lover's prime rib roast, and a must-have for any special occasion. If you find yourself with leftovers, then, by all means, make sandwiches. They will be the best you have ever had.

1. Prepare the grill for medium-high heat with indirect cooking.

2. Trim off any straggling pieces of meat or fat from the roast. If the fat cap is too thick, cut it down to between ¼ to ½ inch (6 to 13 mm) in thickness depending on how you like your prime rib. Run a long sword skewer through the center of the roast lengthwise to create a pilot hole. Run the rotisserie rod through the hole and secure with the forks. Balance as necessary.

3. To make the rub: Combine the rub ingredients in a small bowl and apply all over the roast. Get as much of the rub on as you can, focusing on the round side of the roast. Let sit, uncovered, at room temperature for 10 to 15 minutes.

4. Place the roast on the preheated grill, set a drip pan underneath, and add 2 cups (470 ml) hot water to the pan. If the pan runs dry during the cooking time, add more water. Cook the roast for 2 to 2½ hours, or until it reaches the desired doneness: 125°F (52°C) for rare, 135°F (57°C) for medium rare, 145°F (63°C) for medium, 155°F (68°C) for medium well, or 165°F (74°C) for well done. The roast will shrink during cooking, so adjust the forks when appropriate.

5. Carefully remove the rotisserie forks and slide the rod out, and then place the roast on a large cutting board. Tent the roast with aluminum foil, place a kitchen towel over the foil, and let the meat rest for 15 to 20 minutes. Cut away the bones first by passing a knife against the bones and cutting through (save the bones for later). Cut the meat into slices ¼ to ⅓ inch (6 to 8 mm) thick.

Classic Prime Rib Roast

One 4-bone prime rib roast (8 to 10 pounds, or 3.6 to 4.5 kg)

Rub

3½ tablespoons (63 g) kosher salt

3 or 4 cloves garlic, minced

1½ tablespoons (23 ml) olive oil

1 tablespoon (6 g) coarsely ground black pepper

Yield: 8 to 10 servings

There is truly nothing better than a well-made prime rib roast. This recipe uses few ingredients but produces a fantastic roast. The key is to season the meat well with salt. Opt for a bone-in roast whenever available. The rib bones help keep the meat moist as it cooks and, well . . . who does not love carving those up and having them the day after? The plain and simple truth is, and do not tell anyone not responsible for doing the actual cooking, the ribs are the best part of any rib roast.

1. Prepare the grill for medium-high heat with indirect cooking.

2. Trim off any straggling pieces of meat or fat from the roast. If the fat cap is too thick, cut it down to between ¼ to ½ inch (6 to 13 mm) in thickness depending on how you like your prime rib. Run a long sword skewer through the center of the roast lengthwise to create a pilot hole. Run the rotisserie rod through the hole and secure with the forks. Balance as necessary. This is a large roast and it is important that it be well balanced.

3. To make the rub: Combine the rub ingredients in a small bowl and apply evenly to the roast. Concentrate the rub on the rounded end and not the cut sides, though it should still get some. The rub will then be on the edges of the slices once the roast has been carved.

4. Place the roast on the preheated grill, set a drip pan underneath, and add 2 cups (470 ml) hot water to the pan if you intend to make gravy; add more water during the cooking time as necessary. Cook the roast for 2 to 2½ hours, or until it is near the desired doneness: 125°F (52°C) for rare, 135°F (57°C) for medium rare, 145°F (63°C) for medium, 155°F (68°C) for medium well, or 165°F (74°C) for well done. The roast will shrink during cooking, so adjust the forks when appropriate.

5. Carefully remove the rotisserie forks and slide the rod out, and then place the roast on a large cutting board. Tent the roast with aluminum foil and let the meat rest for 15 to 20 minutes. The roast temperature will continue to rise an additional 5°F (2°C) during the rest phase. Cut away the bones first by passing a knife against the bones and cutting through (save the bones for later). Cut the meat into slices ⅓ to ½ inch (8 to 13 mm) thick.

HORSERADISH-CRUSTED PRIME RIB ROAST

One 4-bone prime rib roast
(8 to 10 pounds, or
3.6 to 4.5 kg)

Rub

⅓ cup (80 g) grated
fresh horseradish root

¼ cup (72 g) kosher salt

¼ cup (60 ml) olive oil

1 tablespoon (6 g) coarsely
ground black pepper

1 tablespoon (15 ml)
white vinegar

1 teaspoon chopped
fresh marjoram

1 teaspoon chopped
fresh thyme

Yield: 8 to 10 servings

Horseradish is the traditional accompaniment for prime rib roast. That earthy heat counterbalances the rich beefy flavor of this fantastic roast. The secret is to skip those jars of flavorless or vinegary horseradish, particularly things labeled "horseradish sauce." We use fresh horseradish root. You should be able to find it in most grocery stores. It looks like a light brown tree root and is just about as dense. Remove the outer skin and finely grate the white flesh of the root.

1. Trim off any straggling pieces of meat or fat from the roast. If the fat cap is too thick, cut it down to between ¼ to ½ inch (6 to 13 mm) in thickness depending on how you like your prime rib.

2. To make the rub: Combine the rub ingredients in a small bowl and coat the roast thoroughly with the mixture. Cover loosely with plastic wrap and let the roast sit at room temperature for 30 minutes.

3. Prepare the grill for medium-high heat with indirect cooking.

4. Run a long sword skewer through the center of the roast lengthwise to create a pilot hole. Run the rotisserie rod through the hole and secure with the forks. Balance as necessary.

5. Place the roast on the preheated grill, set a drip pan underneath, and add 1 to 2 cups (235 to 470 ml) hot water to the pan, adding more water to the pan as needed.

6. Cook the roast for 2 to 2½ hours, or until it is near the desired doneness: 125°F (52°C) for rare, 135°F (57°C) for medium rare, 145°F (63°C) for medium, 155°F (68°C) for medium well, or 165°F (74°C) for well done. The roast will shrink during cooking, so adjust the forks when appropriate.

7. Carefully remove the rotisserie forks and slide the rod out, and then place the roast on a large cutting board. Tent the roast with aluminum foil and let the meat rest for 15 to 20 minutes. The roast temperature will continue to rise an additional 5°F (2°C) during the rest phase. Cut away the bones first by passing a knife against the bones and cutting through (save the bones for later). Cut the meat into thin slices.

Shallot–Grain Mustard Prime Rib Roast

One 4-bone prime rib roast (8 to 10 pounds, or 3.6 to 4.5 kg)

Rub

½ cup (90 g) grainy mustard

¼ cup (60 ml) olive oil

1 large shallot, finely chopped

3 tablespoons (54 g) kosher salt

1½ tablespoons (4.5 g) chopped fresh marjoram

1 tablespoon (3 g) chopped fresh thyme

1 tablespoon (6 g) coarsely ground black pepper

Yield: 8 to 10 servings

Prime rib is the king of roasts and our favorite when the budget allows. When we suggest to people that they take their prime rib out of the oven and put it on a rotisserie on the grill, we get some fearful looks. It seems like a big risk with an expensive cut of beef, but if you are going to cook a prime rib, you should get as much flavor out of it as possible. You can even add a little smoky flavor if so inclined.

1. Trim off any straggling pieces of meat or fat from the roast. If the fat cap is too thick, cut it down to between ¼ to ½ inch (6 to 13 mm) in thickness depending on how you like your prime rib.

2. To make the rub: Combine the rub ingredients in a small bowl and coat the roast thoroughly with it. Loosely cover with plastic wrap and let the roast sit at room temperature for 30 minutes.

3. Prepare the grill for medium-high heat with indirect cooking.

4. Run a long sword skewer through the center of the roast lengthwise to create a pilot hole. Run the rotisserie rod through the hole and secure with the forks. Balance as necessary.

5. Place the roast on the preheated grill, set a drip pan underneath, and add 1 to 2 cups (235 to 470 ml) hot water to the pan. Add more water to the pan as necessary.

6. Cook the roast for about 2 hours, or until it is near the desired doneness: 125°F (52°C) for rare, 135°F (57°C) for medium rare, 145°F (63°C) for medium, 155°F (68°C) for medium well, or 165°F (74°C) for well done. The roast will shrink during cooking, so adjust the forks when appropriate. Remove the roast when it is 5°F to 10°F (2 to 4°C) below the desired doneness. It will continue to cook during the resting phase.

7. Carefully remove the rotisserie forks and slide the rod out, and then place the roast on a large cutting board. Tent the roast with aluminum foil and a kitchen towel and let the meat rest for 15 to 20 minutes. Cut away the bones first by passing a knife against the bones and cutting through (save the bones for later). Cut the meat into thin slices.

WHISKEY-BASTED PRIME RIB ROAST

One 4-bone prime rib roast (8 to 10 pounds, or 3.6 to 4.5 kg)

Rub

¼ cup (72 g) coarse salt

1 small shallot, finely chopped

2 cloves garlic, minced

2 tablespoons (30 ml) olive oil

1 tablespoon (6 g) coarsely ground black pepper

Zest of 1 large lemon

1 teaspoon paprika

1 teaspoon sugar

The addition of whiskey brightens and adds another level of beefiness to this roast. Dab on the baste to keep the seasonings in place. The whiskey will add moisture to the surface of the roast, but should not wash away the crust. The best prime rib is dark and crusted on the surface, so watch the cooking temperature to get it there at the same time that the internal temperature reaches your desired doneness.

---

1. Prepare the grill for medium-high heat with indirect cooking.

2. Trim off any straggling pieces of meat or fat from the roast. If the fat cap is too thick, cut it down to between ¼ to ½ inch (6 to 13 mm) in thickness depending on how you like your prime rib.

3. Run a long sword skewer through the center of the roast lengthwise to create a pilot hole. Run the rotisserie rod through the hole and secure with the forks. Balance as necessary.

4. To make the rub: Combine the rub ingredients in a small bowl to form an even paste. Use additional olive oil if necessary to get it to a thick but workable consistency. Apply evenly to the roast, focusing on the outer shell of the roast.

Baste

⅓ cup (80 ml) whiskey

¼ cup (60 ml) water

Juice of 1 lemon

⅛ teaspoon salt

Yield: 8 to 10 servings

5. To make the baste: Combine the baste ingredients in a small bowl and set aside for 15 to 30 minutes to come to room temperature.

6. Place the roast on the preheated grill, set a drip pan underneath, and add 1 to 2 cups (235 to 470 ml) hot water to the pan. If you intend to make a gravy from the drippings, monitor the drip pan to make sure it does not run dry. Add extra water if needed.

7. Cook the roast for 2 to 2½ hours. During the last hour of cooking time, begin basting. Apply the baste gently so as not to wash away the seasonings on the outside of the roast. Do this 6 to 8 times, until the roast is well coated with the baste. Cook until it is near the desired doneness: 125°F (52°C) for rare, 135°F (57°C) for medium rare, 145°F (63°C) for medium, 155°F (68°C) for medium well, or 165°F (74°C) for well done. The roast will shrink during cooking, so adjust the forks when appropriate.

8. Carefully remove the rotisserie forks and slide the rod out, and then set the roast on a large cutting board. Tent the roast with aluminum foil and let the meat rest for 15 to 20 minutes. Cut away the bones first by passing a knife against the bones and cutting through (save the bones for later). Cut the meat into thin slices.

ROSEMARY–RED WINE PRIME RIB ROAST

Rub

3 to 3½ tablespoons (54 to 63 g) kosher salt

1 tablespoon (2 g) finely chopped fresh rosemary

2 or 3 cloves garlic, minced

2 teaspoons freshly ground black pepper

1 boneless prime rib roast, 4 to 5 pounds (1.8 to 2.3 kg)

Baste

1 cup (235 ml) Cabernet Sauvignon

½ cup (120 ml) low-sodium beef broth

1½ teaspoons soy sauce

1½ teaspoons Worcestershire sauce

Yield: 8 to 10 servings

This rib roast is coated in a savory rosemary rub and basted with red wine, which flavors, tenderizes, and makes this prime rib fantastic. It is not too overpowering, but it is reminiscent of a good braising. We highly recommend a high-quality Cabernet Sauvignon for this recipe. The drippings make an excellent gravy or can be used for a drip pan vegetable dish.

1. To make the rub: Combine the rub ingredients in a small bowl and mix well. Use the salt to grind the garlic and rosemary together.

2. Run a long sword skewer through the center of the roast lengthwise to create a pilot hole. Run the rotisserie rod through the hole and secure with the forks. Balance as necessary.

3. Apply the rub to the roast. Cover with plastic wrap and set in a safe place at room temperature for 30 minutes (rotisserie rod and all).

4. To make the baste: Combine the baste ingredients in a small bowl and store in the refrigerator until ready to use. It will separate, so stir occasionally. Warm the baste for 30 seconds to 1 minute in the microwave before applying to the roast.

5. Prepare the grill for medium-high heat with indirect cooking.

6. Place the roast on the preheated grill, set a drip pan underneath, and add 1 to 2 cups (235 to 470 ml) hot water to the pan. Cook for up to 2 hours, basting intermittently during the last half of the cooking time, until it reaches the desired doneness: 125°F (52°C) for rare, 135°F (57°C) for medium rare, 145°F (63°C) for medium, 155°F (68°C) for medium well, or 165°F (74°C) for well done. The roast will shrink during cooking, so adjust the forks when appropriate.

7. Carefully remove the rotisserie forks and slide the rod out, and then set the roast on a large cutting board. Tent the roast with aluminum foil and let the meat rest for 15 to 20 minutes. Slice and serve.

Churrasco Beef

Marinade

¼ cup (60 ml) olive oil

¼ cup (60 ml) red wine vinegar

2 cloves garlic, smashed

2 teaspoons kosher salt

2 teaspoons onion powder

1 teaspoon freshly ground black pepper

1 sirloin roast with the fat intact, about 4 pounds (1.8 kg)

Yield: 8 servings

Across the United States and increasingly around the world, Brazilian barbecue restaurants have become a favorite of millions of people. Servers dressed as Brazilian gauchos walk about with skewers of meat and serve patrons at the table. One of the most popular of these foods is this rotisserie-style beef. Ideally cooked over charcoal, churrasco is a smoky, wonderful dish. Our version maximizes tenderness and scales the cuts for your backyard grill so you too can enjoy this dish anytime.

1. To make the marinade: Combine the marinade ingredients in a small bowl and let sit at room temperature for 10 to 15 minutes.

2. Cut the roast into even thirds and place it into a large resealable plastic bag. Pour in the marinade, release air from the bag, seal, and, in light squeezing motions, work the marinade all over the meat. Refrigerate for 4 to 6 hours.

3. Prepare the grill for high heat with indirect cooking with a drip pan in place.

4. Remove the meat from the marinade and place on a large cutting board. Roll each piece into a "C" shape with the fat on the outside. Run a long sword skewer through each piece in two places toward the ends to create pilot holes. Thread the pieces onto the rotisserie rod and secure tightly. If you stand the rotisserie rod on one end it should look like three Cs. Tie if necessary to hold the roasts in place. These pieces will shrink as they cook and the centerpiece may stop turning. It may be necessary to retighten everything during the cooking process.

5. Place the roast on the preheated grill with the meat directly over the drip pan. Cook for 30 to 45 minutes, until the meat reaches the desired temperature, around 135°F (57°C) for medium rare.

6. Carefully remove the rotisserie forks and slide the rod out, then place the meat on a cutting board and cover with aluminum foil and then a kitchen towel. Let the meat rest for 8 to 10 minutes before carving. Cut into thin slices against the grain and serve.

Porcini-Dusted Top Sirloin Roast

Wet Rub

½ cup (20 g) dried porcini mushrooms

¼ cup (60 ml) olive oil

4 teaspoons (24 g) salt

1 tablespoon (2 g) chopped fresh thyme

2 cloves garlic, minced

1 teaspoon onion powder

1 teaspoon chili powder

1 teaspoon coarsely ground black pepper

1 top sirloin roast, 4 to 4½ pounds (1.8 to 2 kg)

Baste

½ cup (20 g) dried porcini mushrooms

1 or 2 cups (235 or 470 ml) boiling water

½ cup (120 ml) red wine (Cabernet Sauvignon recommended)

1 tablespoon wet rub mixture

1 teaspoon Worcestershire sauce

Porcini gravy (optional, recipe follows)

Yield: 8 servings

Some people think an elegant meal cannot come from the grill. This top sirloin roast has a deep, rich flavor and a fantastic gravy to accompany the meat at the table.

1. For the wet rub: Chop the mushrooms into small pieces. Place in a clean spice or coffee grinder and grind to a fine powder. Transfer to a bowl and add the remaining rub ingredients. Remove 1 tablespoon (6 g) of the mixture and set aside.

2. If the sirloin roast is loose or uneven, tie it with kitchen twine to hold it to a consistent and even shape. Run a long sword skewer through the center of the roast lengthwise to create a pilot hole. Run the rotisserie rod through the hole and secure with the forks. Balance as necessary. Apply the wet rub evenly to the meat.

3. Prepare the grill for medium-high heat with indirect cooking.

4. Place the roast on the preheated grill, set a drip pan underneath, and add 1 to 2 cups (235 to 470 ml) hot water to the pan. Cook for about 2 hours, or to the desired doneness: 125°F (52°C) for rare, 135°F (57°C) for medium rare, 145°F (63°C) for medium, 155°F (68°C) for medium well, or 165°F (74°C) for well done. Adjust the forks when appropriate.

5. While the roast cooks, make the baste: Add the dried porcini mushrooms to 1 cup (235 ml) boiling water, or 2 cups (470 ml) boiling water if you would like to use the porcini broth for the gravy. Steep the mushrooms for 30 minutes, covered. Strain the broth and reserve the porcinis (for the gravy) and broth separately. Divide the broth into two equal portions, one for the baste and one for the gravy. Combine 1 cup (235 ml) broth with remaining baste ingredients. Let sit for 15 to 30 minutes to come to room temperature before using. Begin basting the roast during the last half of the cooking time and repeat every 10 to 12 minutes until the roast is ready.

6. Carefully remove the rotisserie forks and slide the rod out. Tent the roast with aluminum foil and let the meat rest for 20 minutes. Cut into ¼-inch (6 mm) slices and serve with the porcini gravy, if desired.

Porcini Gravy

1 tablespoon (15 ml) olive oil

3 tablespoons (30 g) finely chopped shallot

1 cup (235 ml) porcini broth (from page 84) or beef broth

½ cup (120 g) reconstituted porcini mushrooms (from page 84), roughly chopped

¼ cup (60 ml) red wine (Cabernet Sauvignon recommended)

2 teaspoons Dijon mustard

½ teaspoon chopped fresh thyme

⅛ teaspoon salt

⅛ teaspoon freshly ground black pepper

1 tablespoon (14 g) unsalted butter

Yield: About 1½ cups (355 ml)

This is an easy and flavorful gravy that perfectly pairs with the Porcini-Dusted Top Sirloin Roast (opposite).

Heat the oil in a medium-size skillet over medium heat. Add the shallot and cook for 3 minutes. Increase the heat to high, add the broth, and bring to a boil. Add the reconstituted porcinis, wine, mustard, thyme, salt, and pepper and stir to combine. Decrease the heat to medium-low and simmer for 12 to 15 minutes, stirring occasionally. Remove the pan from the heat and stir in the butter.

Coffee-Crusted Sirloin Roast

1 sirloin roast,
3 pounds (1.4 kg)

Rub

2 tablespoons (12 g)
ground espresso

3 or 4 cloves garlic, minced

1½ tablespoons (23 ml)
balsamic vinegar

1 tablespoon (15 ml) olive oil

1 tablespoon (18 g) kosher salt

2 teaspoons onion powder

2 teaspoons freshly
ground black pepper

1 teaspoon
Worcestershire sauce

Yield: 6 servings

Don't be alarmed by using coffee in a seasoning rub. It won't taste like burnt coffee, but it will combine with the other spices to produce a deep, earthy flavor. This is particularly good with beef, as it kicks up the natural flavors and produces a delicious end product. Save the leftovers for sandwiches. You'll be glad you did!

---

1. Preheat the grill for medium-high heat with indirect cooking.

2. Pat the roast dry with paper towels. Run a long sword skewer through the center of the roast lengthwise to create a pilot hole. Run the rotisserie rod through the hole and secure with the forks. Balance as necessary.

3. To make the rub: Combine the rub ingredients and apply all over the meat. Tie the roast with twine to create a uniform shape.

4. Place the roast on the preheated grill, set a drip pan underneath, and add 1 to 2 cups (235 to 470 ml) hot water to the pan, adding more water as necessary. Cook the roast for 60 to 70 minutes, or until the meat reaches the desired doneness: 125°F (52°C) for rare, 135°F (57°C) for medium rare, 145°F (63°C) for medium, 155°F (68°C) for medium well, or 165°F (74°C) for well done. The roast will shrink during cooking, so adjust the forks when appropriate.

5. Carefully remove the rotisserie forks and slide the rod out, and then set the roast on a large cutting board. Tent the roast with aluminum foil and let the meat rest for 15 to 20 minutes. Cut off the twine. Slice and serve. If using for sandwiches, slice the meat as thinly as possible.

BALSAMIC-GLAZED CHUCK ROAST

Glaze

¾ cup (180 ml) balsamic vinegar

3 tablespoons (45 g) packed brown sugar

½ teaspoon Worcestershire sauce

1 chuck roast, 3 to 3½ pounds (1.4 to 1.6 kg)

Rub

2 teaspoons kosher salt

1½ teaspoons onion powder

1 teaspoon freshly ground black pepper

½ teaspoon garlic powder

Yield: 6 servings

The chuck roast is an incredibly flavorful and economical cut of beef. Dressed up a little with a balsamic and brown sugar glaze, it is perfect served as the main attraction or added to beef dip sandwiches or hearty salads. Keep in mind that chuck roast does contain internal knobs of fat that can only be trimmed away after it has cooked.

1. To make the glaze: Combine the glaze ingredients in a saucepan over medium heat and simmer for 5 to 6 minutes, stirring often. Watch for burning and decrease the heat if necessary. The mixture should be runny as this is really more of a mop than a thick glaze. Cover the pot and remove from the heat. Allow to cool.

2. Cut away any lumps of excess fat from the surface of the roast. Lay the roast out on a large cutting board. With kitchen twine and starting in the center, tie the roast into a round shape. This means tying it tightly, but it will come into shape as you tie. This will take about five ties to get the proper round roast. Run a long sword skewer through the center of the roast lengthwise to create a pilot hole. Run the rotisserie rod through the hole and secure with the forks. Balance as necessary.

3. Prepare the grill for medium-high heat with indirect cooking.

4. To make the rub: Combine the rub ingredients in a small bowl and apply all over the roast.

5. Place the roast on the preheated grill and set a drip pan underneath. Cook for 50 to 70 minutes, depending on your preferred doneness: 125°F (52°C) for rare, 135°F (57°C) for medium rare, 145°F (63°C) for medium, 155°F (68°C) for medium well, or 165°F (74°C) for well done. After the first 25 minutes of cooking, begin generously basting with the glaze every 10 minutes until the roast is done.

6. Remove from the heat, carefully remove the rotisserie forks and slide the rod out, and then set the roast on a large cutting board. Tent the roast with aluminum foil and let the meat rest for 10 to 15 minutes. Cut off the twine. Cut the meat into ⅓- to ½-inch (8 to 13 mm) slices and serve.

Chipotle Barbacoa Chuck Roast

Marinade

1 (7-ounce, or 196 g) can chipotle peppers in adobo

1 cup (160 g) diced onion

½ cup (120 ml) beef or vegetable broth

3 cloves garlic, cut into fourths

1 tablespoon (6 g) ground cumin

2 tablespoons (30 ml) water

1 tablespoon (15 ml) white vinegar

1 tablespoon (18 g) salt

2 teaspoons dried oregano

We love that savory, slightly spicy shredded beef you find in many fast casual Mexican restaurants. After some experimenting, we came up with this dramatically improved version. For our barbacoa we chose a large chuck roast because the fat keeps the meat moist and tender and because it is a relatively inexpensive beef cut. Keep in mind that chuck roast does contain internal knobs of fat that can only be trimmed away after it has cooked. This star attraction can be sliced and served alone or added to tacos, burritos, or enchiladas. Served up with refried beans and rice it makes quite a tasty meal.

---

1. To make the marinade: Place the marinade ingredients in a food processor and pulse 8 to 10 times. Everything should be very finely chopped and combined. Reserve 1 cup (235 g) of the mixture to use as a baste and refrigerate until ready to cook, then bring to room temperature before using.

2. Trim away any loose or excess pieces of fat from the roast. Place in a large glass dish or large resealable plastic bag. Pour the marinade over the meat, making sure all sides are well covered. Seal the bag or cover the dish with plastic wrap and place in the refrigerator for 12 to 24 hours.

3. Prepare the grill for medium to medium-high heat with indirect cooking.

1 chuck roast, 3½ to 4 pounds
(1.6 to 1.8 kg)

Yield: 6 to 8 servings

4. Remove the roast from the bag, discarding the marinade. Lay the roast out on a large cutting board. With kitchen twine, tie the roast into a round and uniform shape, pulling tightly. Start in the center and work toward the ends until it is tied into a solid round roast. This will take four or five ties. Run a long sword skewer through the center of the roast lengthwise to create a pilot hole. Run the rotisserie rod through the hole and secure with the forks. Balance as necessary.

5. Place the roast on the preheated grill and set a drip pan underneath. Cook for 2 to 3 hours, or until the meat reaches an internal temperature of about 160°F (71°C). Baste with the reserved marinade during the last 30 to 40 minutes of cooking. This roast is intentionally overcooked so that it can be shredded easily. It will be tender and juicy.

6. Remove from the heat, carefully remove the rotisserie forks and slide the rod out, and then set the roast on a large cutting board. Tent the roast with aluminum foil and let the meat rest for 20 minutes. Cut off the twine. Shred into small pieces or carve into thin slices and serve with warmed tortillas, Spanish rice, beans, and fresh salsa.

PORT-SHALLOT CHUCK ROAST

Marinade

1 tablespoon (15 ml) olive oil

1 shallot, finely chopped

2 or 3 cloves garlic, minced

1½ cups (355 ml) tawny port

¼ cup (60 ml) beef broth

1½ tablespoons (23 ml) balsamic vinegar

1 teaspoon Worcestershire sauce

1 teaspoon chopped fresh thyme

¼ teaspoon salt

¼ teaspoon freshly ground black pepper

As we've said, chuck roast is a delicious yet economical cut of beef. We dress this one up with a port-shallot baste that makes this dish reminiscent of braised beef or a fancy pot roast. Use the leftovers in sandwiches or soups. It's perfectly seasoned and ready to be used in multiple recipes. Keep in mind that chuck roast does contain internal knobs of fat that can only be trimmed away after it has cooked.

1. To make the marinade: Heat the olive oil in a saucepan over medium-low heat and cook the shallot for 3 minutes until translucent. Add the garlic and cook for 30 seconds. Increase the heat to medium-high and add the port. Stir thoroughly and cook for 1 minute. Add the remaining ingredients and simmer the sauce for 5 minutes, stirring occasionally. Remove from the heat and let cool for 10 to 15 minutes. Divide the mixture into two even portions, reserving one half for the baste and one for the marinade. Store in the refrigerator until ready to cook, then bring to room temperature before using.

2. Trim away excess fat from the outer edges of the chuck roast. Place the roast in a resealable plastic bag. Add half of the port mixture to the bag, making sure that all of the meat is well covered. Seal the bag and place in the refrigerator for 6 to 8 hours.

3. Prepare the grill for medium-high heat with indirect cooking.

1 chuck roast, 4 to 4½ pounds (1.8 to 2 kg)

1¼ teaspoons salt

½ teaspoon freshly ground black pepper

Yield: 8 servings

4. Remove the roast from the bag, discarding the marinade, and place on a large cutting board or platter. With kitchen twine, tie the roast into a round and uniform shape, pulling tightly. Start in the center and work toward the ends until it is tied into a solid round roast. This will take four or five ties. Run a long sword skewer through the center of the roast lengthwise to create a pilot hole. Run the rotisserie rod through the hole and secure with the forks. Balance as necessary. Season the roast with the salt and pepper.

5. Place the roast on the preheated grill and set an empty drip pan underneath. Cook for 50 to 70 minutes, depending on your preferred doneness: 125°F (52°C) for rare, 135°F (57°C) for medium rare, 145°F (63°C) for medium, 155°F (68°C) for medium well, or 165°F (74°C) for well done. Baste halfway through the cooking time, and repeat the process at least 3 times until the roast is done.

6. Remove from the heat, carefully remove the rotisserie forks and slide the rod out, and then set the roast on a large cutting board. Tent the roast with aluminum foil and let the meat rest for 15 to 20 minutes. Cut off the twine. Slice into ¼-inch (6 mm) slices and serve.

Beef Tenderloin

1 beef tenderloin,
3 to 3½ pounds (1.4 to 1.6 kg)

1 tablespoons (15 ml) olive oil

Rub

2 teaspoons salt

2 teaspoons freshly
ground black pepper

½ teaspoon paprika

½ teaspoon herbes
de Provence

Yield: 6 servings

Imagine filet mignon. Now imagine a roast of filet mignon. Yes, this is an investment, but well worth the price. Our recommendation is not to cook this roast past medium, so if you like your beef well done, you might not want to use this recipe. Anything beyond medium will lead to a dry and tough roast. However, at medium rare, this is absolutely fantastic. The secret with this roast is what is referred to as a reverse sear, which is a little bit of a challenge on a rotisserie, but not as complicated as you might think. What this means is that the roast gets slowly brought up to around 100°F (38°C) before we turn up the heat and sear the surface as quickly as possible. This is easiest on a gas grill or a grill with an infrared rotisserie burner, but it can be done over charcoal as well. To take this to an elegant level, serve with Pancetta Jam (page 94), Porcini Gravy (page 85), or Beurre Blanc (page 66).

1. Prepare the grill for medium heat with indirect cooking.

2. Rub the roast with the oil.

3. To make the rub: Combine the rub ingredients in a small bowl and apply all over the roast.

4. Tie any loose pieces of the roast with kitchen twine. Run a long sword skewer through the center of the roast lengthwise to create a pilot hole. Run the rotisserie rod through the hole and secure with the forks. Balance as necessary.

5. Place the roast on the preheated grill, set a drip pan underneath, and add 1 cup (235 ml) hot water to the pan. When the roast reaches an internal temperature of 100°F (38°C), about 30 minutes, it is time to increase the grill temperature to high. Start by removing the drip pan. On a gas grill with standard burners, light the burners under the roast and turn them to high. On a grill with a rotisserie burner, turn that burner to high. When using a charcoal grill, remove the lid and carefully move the coals directly under the roast. Open the vents completely. It may be necessary to add extra pre-lit charcoal. This is best accomplished by having the coals already burning in a charcoal chimney. Add these slowly to prevent sparking and ash from reaching the roast.

6. Watch the grill and roast closely from this point forward. Look for flare-ups and burning. If you experience flare-ups do not douse with water. Simply place the drip pan under the roast and add 2 cups (470 ml) hot water to prevent the pan from burning through. Continue cooking until the internal temperature at the center reaches your desired doneness: 125°F (52°C) for rare, 135°F (57°C) for medium rare, 145°F (63°C) for medium, 155°F (68°C) for medium well, or 165°F (74°C) for well done.

7. Remove from the heat, carefully remove the rotisserie forks and slide the rod out, and then set the meat on a large cutting board. Tent the roast with aluminum foil and let the meat rest for 15 to 20 minutes. Cut off the twine. Slice and serve.

Pancetta Jam

6 ounces (168 g) pancetta
(or bacon)

1 cup (160 g) finely
chopped sweet onion

2 cloves garlic, minced

1 cup (225 g) packed
brown sugar

¼ cup (60 ml) maple syrup

2 tablespoons (30 ml)
rendered pancetta fat

2 tablespoons (30 ml)
balsamic vinegar

2 teaspoons white
wine vinegar

1 teaspoon
Worcestershire sauce

½ teaspoon freshly
ground black pepper

¼ teaspoon salt

Yield: About 1 cup (240 g)

Although this can be made with bacon, the more subtle flavor of pancetta gives the other ingredients a chance to shine. We have to say that trying this recipe was a complete surprise. Yes, a jam made with what is basically the Italian version of bacon sounds a little strange, even for us, but once this came together we could not stop sampling it. It is sweet. It is salty. It is absolutely fantastic. Small amounts of this will go a long way, but we promise you that it will not sit around for very long. This is the perfect topping for all manner of dishes, but works particularly well on our Beef Tenderloin (page 92) as well as any grilled or rotisserie beef, pork, or chicken.

1. Fry the pancetta in a skillet over medium-high heat until crispy, about 4 minutes, then remove from the skillet, reserving the fat, and drain on paper towels. Chop into fine pieces. Measure 2 tablespoons (30 ml) of the rendered fat to keep in the pan and discard the rest.

2. Turn the heat to medium-low, add the onion, and sauté for 5 minutes. Add the minced garlic and sauté for 15 to 20 seconds. Add the remaining ingredients, including the pancetta, increase the heat to medium-high, and cook for 1 minute, stirring constantly. Decrease the heat to medium and simmer for 5 minutes. Decrease the heat to low and simmer for 15 minutes, stirring often. The jam should be quite thick and chunky at this point.

3. Remove from the heat and let cool for 5 minutes, and then serve. If making ahead of time, reheat the jam before serving. It will become very sticky. Store the jam in the refrigerator in an airtight container for up to 5 days.

Rotisserie Roast Beef

Rub

2 tablespoons (36 g)
kosher salt

2 teaspoons freshly
ground black pepper

1 teaspoon onion powder

¼ teaspoon garlic powder

1 eye of round beef roast, 4 to
5 pounds (1.8 to 2.3 kg)

Yield: 8 to 10 servings

Roast beef is one of the best ingredients for a great sandwich. The problem is getting a roast beef that is not dry and tough. The rotisserie has proven to be our favorite method here. The roast cooks more quickly and self-bastes. If you prefer, you can throw in some smoke for a little extra flavor (see page 22). This roast is easy enough to cook periodically just for delicious sandwiches. Be patient, slice it very thin, and there will be no more fast-food roast beef sandwiches in your future.

---

1. Prepare the grill for medium-high heat with indirect cooking.

2. To make the rub: Combine all the rub ingredients in a small bowl. Season the meat on all sides with the rub. Be sure to apply some to the ends.

3. Run a long sword skewer through the center of the roast lengthwise to create a pilot hole. Run the rotisserie rod through the hole and secure with the forks. Balance as necessary.

4. Place the roast on the preheated grill, set a drip pan underneath, and add 2 cups (470 ml) hot water to the pan. If you intend to catch the drippings for gravy, make sure that the water pan does not run dry and the drippings burn. Cook for 1½ to 2 hours; the ideal internal temperature to pull the roast from the grill is 140°F (60°C) for medium rare to medium. The temperature will continue to climb during the resting phase. The roast will shrink during cooking, so adjust the forks when appropriate.

5. Remove from the heat, carefully remove the rotisserie forks and slide the rod out, and then set the roast on a large cutting board. Tent the roast with aluminum foil and let the meat rest for 20 to 25 minutes. The resting time is key. This will help the juices redistribute and create a more tender and flavorful roast beef.

6. Using a sharp knife, cut the roast into very thin slices. If you have a meat slicer, then the process will be much quicker. Use in sandwiches, wraps, or salads, or roll into cylinders and serve with horseradish sauce for the perfect appetizer.

CHAPTER 3

PORK

Pork is an amazing and often underappreciated meat. The tenderloin is a completely different meat from the pork butt (also known as a Boston roast). The texture and flavor variation makes us wonder how this meat is from the same animal. As a rotisserie item, pork offers everything from a fast roast to low and slow traditional barbecue (try our rotisserie method for pulled pork). Remember that larger cuts of pork can take the heat, as the fat keeps it moist, and they work well with most flavor profiles.

It is hard to say what our favorite cut for pork is, since we cook everything from ribs to hams on the rotisserie. Ribs will come off the rotisserie like they spent hours in the smoker. We love putting a whole, bone-in ham on the rotisserie to first warm it through, and then turn up the heat to glaze it to crunchy, candy-coated perfection. Pork butt is another particular favorite because its fat content ensures a juicy and tender roast.

One of the best bits of news received in the last few years is that due to improvements in pork quality, the USDA has changed the recommended cooking temperature from 165°F (74°C) to 145°F (63°C). This means that pork is now safely cooked to medium instead of well done, so no more dried-out pork roasts. That little hint of pink in the middle makes all the difference in the world. Our cooking instructions follow these new guidelines, and, while the finished temperature is up to you, we fully encourage you to take the temperature down on cuts like loin and tenderloin and taste the difference for yourself.

ROTISSERIE PULLED PORK

1 pork butt, 5 to 6 pounds
(2.3 to 2.7 kg)

Rub

2 tablespoons (12 g) paprika

2 tablespoons (30 g)
packed brown sugar

1 tablespoon (18 g) kosher salt

1 tablespoon (8 g) mild
chili powder

1 teaspoon freshly
ground black pepper

1 teaspoon celery salt

½ teaspoon cayenne

½ teaspoon garlic powder

Yield: 10 servings

Love pulled pork? Well, this recipe will produce a tender, flavorful version without a smoker or slow cooker. You'll be amazed at how well this works. We recommend using with our barbecue sauce (page 63) and serving with a creamy coleslaw.

1. Prepare the grill for medium-low heat with indirect cooking. Prepare to produce smoke during the cooking process (see page 22).

2. Run a long sword skewer through the center of the roast lengthwise to create a pilot hole. Run the rotisserie rod through the hole and secure with the forks. Balance as necessary.

3. To make the rub: Combine the rub ingredients in a small bowl and apply evenly all over the roast. Let sit at room temperature for 15 minutes. By this time the grill should be ready.

4. Place the roast on the grill with a drip pan underneath. Cook until the internal temperature reaches 185°F (85°C), about 6 hours. The roast will shrink during cooking, so adjust the forks when appropriate.

5. Remove from the heat, carefully remove the rotisserie forks and slide the rod out, and then set the pork on a large cutting board. Tent the roast with aluminum foil and let the meat rest for 20 minutes. Remove the foil and let stand for an additional 10 minutes.

6. Using two forks, check to see how easily the meat shreds. Some parts will do this more easily than others. Be sure to use heat-resistant gloves to break the roast apart. Begin shredding each large chunk one at a time. Add pieces to a large bowl and either add the barbecue sauce directly to the shredded meat or serve on the side. Keep the bowl covered as you're working on each section. This will help keep the meat warm. Serve by itself or with your favorite sides or in sandwiches.

Truffle and Herb Bone-In Pork Roast

One 8- to 10-bone
pork loin roast

1 recipe Pork Brine (page 51)

Rub

1 truffle, finely chopped,
or 2 tablespoons (20 g)
truffle pieces

½ cup (1 stick, 112 g) unsalted
butter, at room temperature

3 cloves garlic, minced

2 tablespoons (4 g)
chopped fresh marjoram

1 tablespoon (10 g)
grated onion

2 teaspoons chopped
fresh thyme

1 teaspoon honey

½ teaspoon apple
cider vinegar

½ teaspoon freshly
ground black pepper

Yield: 8 servings

This is an economical cut of pork with a fancy flair. Serve this decadent pork rib roast on special occasions. If you cannot locate jarred truffle pieces, then by all means use fresh truffles. One truffle is more than enough for this recipe, so it will not be a huge investment.

1. Brine the pork roast in a large container in the refrigerator for 4 hours. Rinse off any excess salt and pat dry with paper towels.

2. To make the rub: If you are using a whole, fresh truffle, lightly toast it in a small skillet. Chop it finely. Combine all the rub ingredients in a small bowl. Mix well into a thick paste. Apply the rub evenly to the roast.

3. Prepare the grill for medium to medium-high heat with indirect cooking.

4. Run a long sword skewer through the center of the roast lengthwise to create a pilot hole. Run the rotisserie rod through the hole and secure with the forks. Balance as necessary.

5. Place the roast on the preheated grill, set a drip pan underneath, and add 2 cups (470 ml) hot water to the pan. Once the roast reaches an internal temperature of 130°F (54°C), it is time to increase the grill temperature to high. Start by removing the drip pan. On a gas grill with standard burners, light the burners under the roast and turn them to high. On a grill with a rotisserie burner, turn that burner to high. When using a charcoal grill, remove the lid and carefully move the coals directly under the roast. Open the vents completely. It may be necessary to add more pre-lit charcoal. This is best accomplished by having the coals already burning in a charcoal chimney. Add these slowly to prevent sparking and ash from reaching the roast. Cook until the roast reaches an internal temperature of 140°F to 145°F (60°C to 63°C). The roast will shrink during cooking, so adjust the forks when appropriate.

6. Remove from the heat, carefully remove the rotisserie forks and slide the rod out, and then set the roast on a large cutting board. Tent the roast with aluminum foil and let the meat rest for 10 minutes. Carve between the bones for the perfect "pork chop" portion size.

Hawaiian Sticky Pork Roast

Sauce

1 cup (235 ml) pineapple juice

1 cup (225 g) packed brown sugar

3 tablespoons (45 ml) soy sauce

1 pork butt roast, 4 to 5 pounds (1.8 to 2.3 kg)

1½ teaspoons sea salt

1 teaspoon white pepper

Yield: 8 to 10 servings

The pork butt, sometimes called a Boston roast, is one of our favorite cuts. When you examine one of these, it might seem a little strange. This rectangular block of pork from the shoulder region has a big bone through the middle and large clumps of fat. It is these factors that give this roast so much flavor and make it perfect for a recipe like this one. Slow roasting on the rotisserie is going to melt away a lot of the fat (so make sure you use a drip pan) and turn the meat into a pile of tender deliciousness. One word of warning. The bone at the heart of this roast presents a small challenge to rotisserie cooking. You will need to find a path through the center for the rod and that might take a few attempts.

1. To make the sauce: Combine the sauce ingredients in a saucepan over medium-high heat and simmer for 2 minutes, stirring often. Decrease the heat to medium-low and simmer for another 4 to 5 minutes. The sauce should be a little runnier than syrup. Remove from the heat and let cool for at least 30 minutes before using. Divide into two equal portions, one for the baste and one to serve alongside the roast.

2. Trim the fat cap on the roast to ½ inch (1.3 cm) thick. Score the fat lightly with a sharp knife in a diagonal pattern.

3. Combine the sea salt and white pepper and apply all over the pork. Let sit for 15 to 20 minutes at room temperature.

4. Prepare the grill for medium heat with indirect cooking.

5. Run a long sword skewer to find the best path through the center of the roast lengthwise to create a pilot hole. Run the rotisserie rod through the hole and secure with the forks. Balance as necessary. If needed, run the rod through diagonally and secure tightly with the rotisserie forks.

6. Place the roast on the preheated grill, set a drip pan underneath, and add 1 cup (235 ml) hot water to the pan. Cook the roast for 3 to 4 hours, or until it reaches 185°F (85°C) in the center. The roast will shrink during cooking, so adjust the forks when appropriate. During the last half of the cooking time, baste with half of the sauce.

7. Remove from the heat, carefully remove the rotisserie forks and slide the rod out, and then set the roast on a large cutting board. Tent the roast with aluminum foil and let the meat rest for 10 to 15 minutes. Slice and place on a platter. Rewarm the reserved sauce in the microwave for 30 seconds to 1 minute and drizzle over the sliced pork. Serve.

Apricot and Chili-Glazed Bone-in Pork Loin Roast

One 5- or 6-bone pork loin roast

1 recipe Pork Brine (page 51)

Glaze

½ cup (115 g) applesauce

½ cup (120 ml) chili sauce

½ cup (115 g) apricot preserves

3 tablespoons (60 g) honey

1 tablespoon (15 ml) soy sauce

Rub

1 teaspoon chili powder

½ teaspoon onion powder

¼ teaspoon sweet paprika

¼ teaspoon dried marjoram

¼ teaspoon garlic powder

¼ teaspoon freshly ground black pepper

⅛ teaspoon ground allspice

Yield: 5 or 6 servings

The bone-in pork loin is the prime rib of pork. Fortunately, it costs considerably less than its beef equivalent, making it the perfect choice for special occasions on a budget. The real secret to making this pork roast delicious is the brine. This adds moisture to the meat and keeps it juicy and tender on the rotisserie.

1. Brine the pork loin roast in a large container in the refrigerator for 4 to 8 hours. Rinse off any excess salt and pat dry with paper towels.

2. To make the glaze: Combine the glaze ingredients in a medium saucepan and bring to a simmer over medium heat. Stir often and watch for burning. Decrease the heat to low. Once the mixture is well combined and has the consistency of maple syrup, remove it from the heat and let cool for at least 5 minutes before using.

3. Prepare the grill for medium-high heat with indirect cooking.

4. To make the rub: Combine the rub ingredients in a small bowl. Season the entire roast with rub.

5. Run a long sword skewer through the center of the roast lengthwise to create a pilot hole. Run the rotisserie rod through the hole and secure with the forks. Balance as necessary.

6. Place the roast on the preheated grill and set a drip pan underneath. Cook the roast, basting with the glaze after the first hour of cooking time, until the internal temperature reaches 140°F (60°C) and the sauce is well caramelized. The roast temperature will continue to rise an additional 5°F (2°C) during the rest phase. The roast will shrink during the cooking process, so adjust the forks when appropriate.

7. Remove from the heat, carefully remove the rotisserie forks and slide the rod out, and then set the roast on a large cutting board. Tent the roast with aluminum foil and let the meat rest for 15 minutes. Slice the roast between the bones, which will provide a nice thick pork chop portion. Serve immediately.

Porchetta

Traditionally, the Italian dish porchetta *refers to a skin-on suckling pig that has been deboned, coated in herbs and spices, tied, and roasted for several hours. The meat is thinly sliced and served on sandwiches or as a main dish. Since its inception, several variations have popped up. You can find porchetta that is simply a large chunk or meat still attached to a thick coating of fat and skin. However, the fat is quite difficult to render and the tough outer skin of an adult pig can sometimes be too dense to eat. For this reason, we are using pork belly to lard the loin roast. This creates a nice outer crispiness with a bit of fat and a lot of flavorful lean pork loin in the center.*

1 slab pork belly, skin on,
5 to 6 pounds (2.3 to 2.7 kg)

1 boneless pork loin roast,
about 3 pounds (1.4 kg)

Rub

2 tablespoons (12 g)
fennel seeds

1 tablespoon (2 g) finely
chopped fresh sage

Zest of 1 lemon

4 or 5 cloves garlic

2 teaspoons coarse salt

2 teaspoons freshly
ground black pepper

1 teaspoon chopped
fresh rosemary

1 teaspoon red pepper flakes

1½ teaspoons coarse salt

1 teaspoon freshly
ground black pepper

Yield: 6 servings

1. Lay the pork belly, skin-side down, on a large cutting board. Place the pork loin on top and roll the pork belly together so that the ends meet. Trim any excess pork belly and loin so that it is a uniform cylinder. Do not tie yet.

2. To make the rub: Using a mortar and pestle or spice grinder, crush the fennel seeds to a medium grind. Combine with the remaining rub ingredients in a small bowl and apply all over the pork loin.

3. Roll the pork loin inside the pork belly and tie with kitchen twine every inch (2.5 cm) into a secure, round bundle. Season the outside of the pork belly with the coarse salt and pepper. Set onto a baking sheet and place in the refrigerator, uncovered, for 24 hours.

4. Prepare the grill for medium to medium-high heat with indirect cooking.

5. Run a long sword skewer through the center of the roast lengthwise to create a pilot hole. Run the rotisserie rod through the hole and secure with the forks. Balance as necessary.

6. Place the porchetta on the grill with a drip pan underneath. Cook for 3 to 4 hours. Watch for burning or excessive browning and adjust the heat as necessary. Once the porchetta has reached an internal temperature of 145°F (63°C), the roast is done. If the skin is not a deep brown and crispy in texture, increase the grill temperature to high for an additional 10 minutes.

7. Remove from the heat, carefully remove the rotisserie forks and slide the rod out, and then set the meat on a large cutting board. Tent the roast with aluminum foil and let the meat rest for 15 minutes. Slice the meat ½ inch (1.3 cm) thick and serve.

Honey-Glazed Ham

Every year people line up to buy candied and glazed hams from specialty stores. You know the ones. The secret to those hams is a sprinkling of sugar that is torched to a hard glaze. We take that one step further by warming the ham on the rotisserie, then glazing it in layers of flavor that caramelizes and candies right on the surface. Hot off the grill, this ham cannot be beat.

Glaze

1½ cups (355 ml) orange juice

½ cup (160 g) honey

2 tablespoons (30 g) packed brown sugar

¼ teaspoon ground cinnamon

⅛ teaspoon ground nutmeg

⅛ teaspoon ground allspice

⅛ teaspoon ground cloves

⅛ teaspoon white pepper

2 tablespoons (28 g) unsalted butter

1 ham, bone in and unsliced, 7 to 8 pounds (3.2 to 3.6 kg)

1 cup (225 g) packed brown sugar

Yield: 12 to 14 servings

1. To make the glaze: Combine the orange juice, honey, brown sugar, and spices in a saucepan and bring almost to a boil over medium-high heat. Decrease the heat to medium and simmer for 10 minutes, stirring often. The mixture should be a little runnier than real maple syrup. Remove from the heat and add the butter, stirring until melted. Let the mixture cool.

2. Prepare the grill for medium heat with indirect cooking.

3. Run a long sword skewer through the center of the ham lengthwise to create a pilot hole. There is a bone in the middle of this ham, but generally it is just to one side. The skewer should easily go through, but feel for the bone before you start so you will know how to navigate around it. Run the rotisserie rod through the hole and secure with the forks. Balance the ham on the rod as well as possible.

4. Place the ham on the preheated grill and set a drip pan underneath, if there is room. The ham should not take too long to heat up—remember, it is precooked—so about 45 minutes should do it. Look for an internal temperature around 130°F (54°C). The surface should be hot.

5. Baste the ham with the glaze after 20 minutes on the grill. Repeat the process every 5 minutes and about 3 more times.

6. During the last 5 to 10 minutes of cooking time, the ham should be hot as well as sticky from the glaze. Turn up the heat to medium-high (adjust the vents on a charcoal grill to be fully open) and sprinkle the brown sugar evenly on the surface of the ham in small amounts until it is completely coated. Continue to cook until the sugar starts to bubble. Move quickly, as sugar tends to burn.

7. Once the sugar is bubbling rapidly, remove the ham from the heat and place on a large cutting board. Remove the rotisserie forks and slide the rod out, loosely cover the ham with aluminum foil, and let it rest for 5 minutes. Carve into thin slices and serve warm.

Apple Butter–Bourbon Ham

1 ham, unsliced, 5 to 6 pounds
(2.3 to 2.7 kg)

Baste

⅓ cup (80 g) apple butter

¼ cup (60 g) packed
brown sugar

2 tablespoons (30 ml) bourbon

1½ teaspoons Dijon mustard

¼ teaspoon ground ginger

¼ teaspoon white pepper

Yield: 10 to 12 servings

The combination of apple butter and bourbon creates a delicious coating for this rotisserie ham. If you are opposed to using bourbon, then use cider vinegar. It will change the flavor a bit, but will serve as a suitable substitute. This recipe can be made any time of the year, but is a definitely a holiday favorite.

1. Prepare the grill for medium-high heat with indirect cooking.

2. Run a long sword skewer through the center of the ham lengthwise to create a pilot hole. Run the rotisserie rod through the hole and secure with the forks. Balance as necessary and secure tightly. Place the ham on the preheated grill and cook for 50 to 60 minutes. If there is room, set a drip pan underneath.

3. To make the baste: Combine all the baste ingredients in a small saucepan and simmer over medium heat for 2 minutes, stirring often. Remove from the heat and let sit for 5 to 10 minutes before using.

4. During the last 20 minutes of the cooking time, begin basting the ham with the apple butter-bourbon mixture. Make at least 4 or 5 passes with the baste to coat evenly. Focus the coating on the outside of the ham and not on the cut side. The ham should not take too long to heat up—remember, it is precooked—so about 45 minutes should do it. Look for an internal temperature around 130°F (54°C). The surface should be hot.

5. Remove from the heat, carefully remove the rotisserie forks and slide the rod out, and then set the ham on a large cutting board. Tent the ham with aluminum foil and let the meat rest for 10 minutes. Carve and serve immediately.

PINEAPPLE-CHERRY GLAZED HAM

Glaze

1 cup (240 g) pineapple preserves

2½ tablespoons (37 g) cherry jelly

2 tablespoons (30 g) packed brown sugar

1 tablespoon (15 ml) water

2 teaspoons soy sauce

1 ham, unsliced, 6 to 7 pounds (2.7 to 3.2 kg)

¼ cup (16 g) whole cloves (use more if necessary)

Yield: 12 to 14 servings

This ham recipe is the revised version of the traditional pineapple, cherry, and clove-studded ham. Since it's quite inconvenient to keep pineapple slices and cherries on the ham as it whirls around on a rotisserie rod, we've improvised a little. We're not saying it can't be done, but you will need a lot—and we mean a lot—of toothpicks, which will burn to cinders on the grill. So, instead of using these items, we have created a comparable glaze. However, the cloves remain.

1. To make the glaze: Combine all the glaze ingredients in a saucepan over low heat and heat through. Do not boil; just bring to a low simmer until everything is melted and well blended. Remove from the heat, cover, and keep warm.

2. Prepare the grill for medium-high heat with indirect cooking.

3. Cut diagonal lines into the surface of the ham in one direction and then again in the opposite direction, creating 1-inch (2.5 cm) squares. Do not cut too deeply. Poke a clove in the center of each square. Run a long sword skewer through the center of the ham lengthwise to create a pilot hole. Run the rotisserie rod through the hole and secure with the forks. Balance as necessary.

4. Place the ham on the preheated grill with a drip pan underneath. Cook for 35 to 40 minutes, basting with the glaze every 5 minutes during the last 20 minutes of cooking time.

5. Remove from the heat, carefully remove the rotisserie forks and slide the rod out, and then set the ham on a large cutting board. Tent the ham with aluminum foil and let the meat rest for 5 to 10 minutes. Plate the ham with the cloves in place, but remove them before carving.

Cuban Pork Tenderloin

2 large pork tenderloins, about 3½ pounds (1.6 kg) each

Marinade

½ cup (120 ml) freshly squeezed orange juice

¼ cup (60 ml) freshly squeezed lime juice

1 tablespoon (15 ml) vegetable oil

3 cloves garlic, grated

½ teaspoon ground cumin

½ teaspoon red pepper flakes

1¼ teaspoons salt

½ teaspoon freshly ground black pepper

2 tablespoons (2 g) chopped fresh cilantro, for garnish

2 limes, quartered, for serving

Yield: 6 servings

Who doesn't love Cuban sandwiches and that delicious citrus flavor of Cuban pork? Since it's difficult to obtain the sour oranges traditionally used in that recipe, we substituted with a blend of regular orange juice and lime juice. Be sure to use freshly squeezed juice for the best results.

1. Cut off any excess fat and remove the silverskin from the tenderloins. Place in a large resealable plastic bag or glass baking dish.

2. To make the marinade: Combine the marinade ingredients in a bowl and pour over the pork. Using tongs, gently turn the pork to coat. Seal the bag or cover the dish with plastic wrap. Place in the refrigerator for 4 to 8 hours. Remove from the refrigerator 30 minutes before you're ready to cook. Drain the tenderloins and pat dry with paper towels.

3. Prepare the grill for medium-high heat with indirect cooking.

4. Place the tenderloins on a large cutting board, large end to small end, making one uniform roast. Season with the salt and pepper. Tie together with kitchen twine every 2 inches (5 cm). Run a long sword skewer through the center of the roasts lengthwise to create a pilot hole. Run the rotisserie rod through the hole and secure with the forks. Balance as necessary.

5. Place the tenderloins on the grill with a drip pan underneath. Cook for 45 to 60 minutes, or until the internal temperature at the thickest part reaches 140°F to 145°F (60°C to 63°C). The roast will shrink during cooking, so adjust the forks when appropriate.

6. Remove from the heat, carefully remove the rotisserie forks and slide the rod out, and then set the tenderloins on a large cutting board. Tent the roast with aluminum foil and let the meat rest for 15 to 20 minutes.

7. Cut away the twine and carve the tenderloins into thin slices. Garnish with the cilantro and serve with the lime wedges.

SAGE AND APPLE PORK LOIN

1 pork loin roast,
3 pounds (1.4 kg)

½ recipe Pork Brine
(page 51)

Rub

1 teaspoon chopped fresh sage

1 teaspoon onion powder

1 teaspoon mustard powder

½ teaspoon sweet paprika

½ teaspoon dried marjoram

½ teaspoon freshly
ground black pepper

¼ teaspoon garlic powder

¼ teaspoon ground nutmeg

¼ teaspoon ground cloves

½ teaspoon chipotle chile
powder (regular chile powder
will also work)

The problem with pork loin is that the meat is very lean. Yes, that is a good thing for the health-conscious, but to keep it moist and tender you'll need to take some extra steps. Our recipe starts with a simple brine. Brines work magic with lean meats like loin. But wait, there is more. This pork loin roast has thin slices of apple placed right into the meat. As the roast cooks, the apples release moisture and flavor.

1. Brine the pork for 4 to 6 hours in a large resealable plastic bag or a plastic or glass container in the refrigerator. Make sure the roast is completely submerged in the brine.

2. To make the rub: Combine all the ingredients in a small bowl and set aside.

3. To make the glaze: Combine all the glaze ingredients in a medium-size saucepan and simmer over medium heat for 5 to 6 minutes, stirring often. Remove from the heat and let cool. Reserve ⅓ cup (80 ml) of the glaze for serving.

4. Prepare the grill for medium-high heat with indirect cooking.

5. Cut the apple in half and core. Cut into thin slices, top to bottom, and then cut the slices in half through the middle, making small, thin apple pieces.

6. Remove the pork from the brine, rinse off the excess salt, and pat dry with paper towels. Make slits into the roast every 2 inches (5 cm). The slit should be smaller on the outside than it is on the inside, making space for the apple slices on the inside, but not allowing them to slip out. Place one apple slice into each slit.

Glaze

½ cup (120 g) apple jelly (not apple butter)

½ cup (120 g) applesauce

3 or 4 large fresh sage leaves, bruised

2 tablespoons (30 ml) apple cider vinegar

2 tablespoons (30 ml) white wine

1 teaspoon Dijon mustard

⅛ teaspoon ground nutmeg

1 Granny Smith apple

Yield: 6 servings

7. Run a long sword skewer through the center of the roast lengthwise to create a pilot hole. Run the rotisserie rod through the hole and secure with the forks. Balance as necessary. Season the roast evenly with the rub.

8. Place the roast on the preheated grill, set a drip pan underneath, and add 1 to 2 cups (235 to 470 ml) hot water to the pan. Cook the roast for 1 to 1½ hours, or until the roast reaches an internal temperature of 165°F (74°C). Baste with the glaze after the first 15 to 20 minutes of cooking time and repeat the process 3 or 4 times until the roast is done. The roast will shrink during cooking, so adjust the forks when appropriate.

9. Remove from the heat, carefully remove the rotisserie forks and slide the rod out, and then set the roast on a large cutting board. Tent the roast with aluminum foil and let the meat rest for 20 minutes. Slice thinly (like a ham) and top with the reserved glaze before serving.

BACON-WRAPPED PORK LOIN

2 pork loins, 2 to 3 pounds (1.8 to 2.3 kg) each

1 recipe Pork Brine (page 51)

Sauce

¼ cup (60 ml) chili sauce

2 tablespoons (30 g) ketchup

1 tablespoon (15 ml) maple syrup

1 tablespoon (15 g) packed brown sugar

2 teaspoons balsamic vinegar

1 teaspoon freshly ground black pepper

½ teaspoon mustard powder

½ teaspoon dried rosemary

¼ teaspoon red pepper flakes

12 strips uncured bacon

Yield: 4 to 6 servings

Pork loin is a great cut. It is relatively inexpensive and loaded with flavor, but it has a tendency to dry out on the grill. It simply does not possess the necessary fat to keep it moist. For this reason, we wrap our pork loin roasts in bacon. It not only adds the necessary fat for self-basting on the rotisserie, but it also offers a little extra smoky flavor to increase the roast's deliciousness.

1. Brine the pork for 2 to 4 hours in a large resealable plastic bag or a plastic or glass container in the refrigerator. Make sure the roasts are completely submerged in the brine.

2. Prepare the grill for medium-high heat with indirect cooking.

3. To make the sauce: Combine all the sauce ingredients in a small bowl, stirring to blend well.

4. Remove the pork from the brine, rinse off the excess salt, and pat dry with paper towels. Place one roast on top of the other on a large cutting board. Brush the surfaces of the meat with the sauce. Place the bacon slices over the roasts running parallel to their length. Some of the sauce will drip off. Do not worry.

5. Tie the roasts together with kitchen twine, securing the bacon slices to the meat. Tie in four or five places, making a single round and uniform roast. Tuck the ends of the roast under the last string on each side.

6. Run a long sword skewer through the center of the roasts lengthwise to create a pilot hole. Run the rotisserie rod through the hole and secure with the forks. Balance as necessary. Place the roast on the preheated grill, set a drip pan underneath, and add 2 cups (470 ml) hot water to the pan. Cook for 90 minutes, or until an internal temperature reaches 140°F (60°C). The roast will shrink during cooking, so adjust the forks when appropriate.

7. Remove from the heat, carefully remove the rotisserie forks and slide the rod out, and then set the pork on a large cutting board. Tent the roast with aluminum foil and a kitchen towel and let the meat rest for 15 minutes. Leave the twine on and use as a guide to cut the roast. This will keep the bacon intact as you carve. Remove the twine as you go.

CHAR SIU PORK
(Chinese Barbecued Pork)

2 pork tenderloins,
about 1½ pounds (680 g) each

Basic Brine (page 50)

Barbecue Glaze

½ cup (120 ml) prepared
sweet and sour sauce

¼ cup (60 ml) hoisin sauce

¼ cup (65 g) packed
light brown sugar

3 tablespoons (45 ml)
soy sauce

1 tablespoon (15 ml)
apple cider vinegar

1 tablespoon (6 g)
minced fresh ginger

2 cloves garlic, minced

2 teaspoons Asian chili paste

½ teaspoon Chinese
five-spice powder

½ teaspoon freshly
ground black pepper

Yield: 6 servings

Char siu is a traditional Cantonese barbecued pork dish that has variations across Asia. There are restaurants that don't just specialize in this incredibly flavorful dish—they sell nothing else. Served over rice, this is a great one-bowl meal, and our rotisserie method means you get to control the amount of smoky flavor. If you want it extra saucy, double the glaze recipe, warm one batch in a saucepan, and pour it over the sliced meat.

1. Brine the pork for 3 to 4 hours in a large resealable plastic bag or a plastic or glass container in the refrigerator. Make sure the meat is completely submerged in the brine.

2. To make the barbecue glaze: Combine the glaze ingredients in a medium-size bowl, stirring until the sugar is dissolved.

3. Prepare the grill for medium-high heat with indirect cooking.

4. Remove the pork from the brine, rinse off the excess salt, and pat dry with paper towels. Place the tenderloins on a large cutting board, large end to small end, making one uniform roast. Tie together with kitchen twine every 2 inches (5 cm). Run a long sword skewer through the center of the roasts lengthwise to create a pilot hole. Run the rotisserie rod through the hole and secure with the forks. Balance as necessary.

5. Place the roast on the preheated grill and set a drip pan underneath. Cook for 1 to 1½ hours, or until the internal temperature reaches 140°F (60°C). Begin applying the glaze after the first 30 minutes of cooking time and repeat the process 3 or 4 times until right before the roast is done. Stop applying the glaze and allow the roast to come to temperature. The roast will shrink during cooking, so adjust the forks when appropriate.

6. Remove from the heat, carefully remove the rotisserie forks and slide the rod out, and then set the roast on a large cutting board. Tent the roast with aluminum foil and let the meat rest for 15 to 20 minutes. Carve into ½-inch (1.3 cm) slices and serve.

Sweet and Sour Pork Tenderloin

Not only is this an old favorite, but it's also quite easy to prepare. Double the baste recipe for a delicious serving sauce. Plate over rice with steamed or drip pan vegetables.

2 large pork tenderloins, 3½ pounds (1.6 kg) each

½ recipe Pork Brine (page 51)

Rub

½ teaspoon white pepper

½ teaspoon ground ginger

½ teaspoon garlic powder

¼ teaspoon ground cloves

Baste

1½ teaspoons vegetable oil

2 cloves garlic, minced

1 cup (225 g) packed brown sugar

1 cup (235 ml) teriyaki sauce

½ cup (120 ml) dry red wine

1 tablespoon (15 ml) apple cider vinegar

Pinch of salt

Yield: 6 servings

1. Brine the pork for 4 to 6 hours in a large resealable plastic bag or a plastic or glass container in the refrigerator.

2. To make the rub: combine the rub ingredients in a small bowl.

3. To make the baste: Heat the oil in a medium-size saucepan over medium heat. Add the garlic and cook for 15 to 20 seconds. Add the remaining baste ingredients. Decrease the heat to medium-low. Gently simmer for 5 minutes, stirring often. Once the sugar has melted, remove from the heat and keep covered. To make a larger portion of serving sauce, double the baste ingredients and follow the cooking instructions. Divide the mixture in half, reserving half to use as a baste, the other half to drizzle on the pork before serving. Reheat if necessary.

4. Prepare the grill for medium-high heat with indirect cooking.

5. Remove the pork from the brine, rinse off the excess salt, and pat dry with paper towels. Place the tenderloins on a large cutting board, large end to small end, making one uniform roast. Tie together with kitchen twine every 2 inches (5 cm). Apply the rub evenly to the meat. Run a long sword skewer through the center of the roasts lengthwise to create a pilot hole. Run the rotisserie rod through the hole and secure with the forks. Balance as necessary.

6. Place the roast on the preheated grill, set a drip pan underneath, and add 1 to 2 cups (235 to 470 ml) hot water to the pan. Cook for 60 to 75 minutes, or until the internal temperature of the thickest part of the meat reaches 140°F (60°C). Begin basting with the sauce after the first 20 minutes of cooking time. Repeat every 8 to 10 minutes until the pork is cooked through. The roast will shrink during cooking, so adjust the forks when appropriate.

7. Remove from the heat, carefully remove the rotisserie forks and slide the rod out, and then set onto a large cutting board. Tent the roast with aluminum foil and let the meat rest for 15 minutes. Cut off the twine and carve into slices ½ inch (1.3 cm) thick. Drizzle with the reserved sauce and serve.

CHINESE-STYLE RIBS

2 racks baby back ribs

Marinade

¾ cup (180 ml) soy sauce

¼ cup (60 ml) dry sherry

¼ cup (60 ml) hoisin sauce

3 tablespoons (45 g)
packed brown sugar

2 tablespoons (40 g) honey

6 cloves garlic, minced

2 tablespoons (30 ml)
white vinegar

1 tablespoon (6 g)
minced fresh ginger

1 tablespoon (14 g)
Asian chili paste

2 teaspoons sesame oil

½ teaspoon Chinese
five-spice powder

½ teaspoon white pepper

½ teaspoon red food
coloring (optional)

1½ tablespoons (12 g)
toasted sesame seeds

2 large scallions, finely sliced

Yield: 4 to 6 servings

Most people throw these classic Chinese-style ribs in the oven, where they pick up no added flavor, but the grill offers so much more. The racks are tied together to make an even and balanced item for the rotisserie. The real secret, however, is the basting, which creates a caramelized sticky layer of flavor.

1. Place the ribs on a cutting board and pat dry with paper towels. Cut away any excess fat from the ribs. Remove the membrane from the back of the ribs by using a blunt knife to work the membrane away from the bone in one corner. Grab hold of the membrane with a paper towel for a good grip and gently peel away. With a little practice, this becomes an easy process.

2. To make the marinade: Combine the marinade ingredients in a medium-size bowl. Reserve ½ cup for basting. Place the ribs into a large resealable bag and add the marinade. Make sure the meat is well coated. Release air from the bag, seal, and place in the refrigerator for 4 to 6 hours.

3. Remove the ribs from the bag, discarding the marinade. Place one rack of ribs meat-side down. Place the second rack bone-side down on top of the first rack, so they are bone to bone, forming an even bundle. Tie securely every other bone with kitchen twine. Pass the rotisserie rod in the space between the two racks. Secure the rod, making sure that the rotisserie forks penetrate the meat in at least two locations on each side.

4. Prepare the grill for medium-high heat with indirect cooking.

5. Place the ribs on the preheated grill and set a drip pan underneath. Begin basting with the reserved marinade after 30 minutes of cooking time and repeat the process every 7 to 10 minutes until the ribs reach an internal temperature of 170°F (77°C). Continue to cook until the internal temperature reaches 175°F (80°C), 1 to 1½ hours total. Test the temperature in several locations.

6. Remove from the heat, carefully remove the rotisserie forks and slide the rod out, and then set the ribs on a large cutting board. Tent the ribs with aluminum foil and let the meat rest for 10 to 15 minutes. Cut away the twine and cut the racks into individual ribs. Garnish with the toasted sesame seeds and sliced scallions.

Memphis-Style Barbecued Ribs

Sauce

1 tablespoon (15 ml) vegetable oil

1 cup (160 g) finely chopped sweet onion

2 cloves garlic, minced

1½ cups (360 g) ketchup

¼ cup (60 ml) red wine vinegar

¼ cup (60 g) packed brown sugar

2 tablespoons (22 g) yellow mustard

⅛ teaspoon salt

In Memphis, pork ribs tend to have a thinner, less sweet barbecue sauce compared to those served in Kansas City. This distinct tradition blends the Deep South's methods with the Midwest's love of tomato-based sauces. To get truly authentic barbecued ribs of this type you need a smoker and about 6 hours of cooking time. We have adapted this method for the grill where the rotisserie ensures even cooking. Although these ribs will get a better quality of smoke from charcoal, a gas grill will still produce amazingly good ribs.

1. To make the sauce: Heat the oil in a medium-size saucepan over medium heat. Add the onions and sauté for 5 minutes. Add the garlic and sauté for 15 seconds. Add the remaining sauce ingredients and simmer for 4 to 5 minutes, stirring often. Remove from the heat and let cool for 15 to 30 minutes before using.

2. Prepare the grill for medium heat with indirect cooking. Prepare to produce smoke during the cooking process (see page 22).

3. To make the rub: Combine the rub ingredients in a small bowl and set aside.

4. Place the ribs on a cutting board and pat dry with paper towels. Cut away any excess fat from the ribs. Remove the membrane from the back of the ribs by using a blunt knife to work the membrane away from the bone in one corner. Grab hold of the membrane with a paper towel for a good grip and gently peel away. With a little practice, this becomes an easy process. Apply the rub all over the ribs' surface, focusing more on the meat side than the bone side.

Rub

1 tablespoon (7 g) paprika

2 teaspoons salt

2 teaspoons freshly
ground black pepper

½ teaspoon cayenne

2 racks baby back ribs

Yield: 4 to 6 servings

5. Place one rack of ribs bone-side up on a large cutting board. Place the other rack of ribs bone-side down on top. Position to match up the racks of ribs as evenly as possible. With kitchen twine, tie the racks together between ever other bone, end to end. The whole bundle should be secure and tight. Run the rotisserie rod between the racks and secure tightly with the rotisserie forks. There will be a little movement in the middle, which is fine. As the ribs cook it may be necessary to tighten the forks to keep them secure. Make sure the forks pass through the meat of each rack on each end.

6. Place the racks on the preheated grill and set a drip pan underneath. Cook for 2 to 3 hours, or until the internal temperature reaches 185°F (85°C). Test the temperature in several locations. Baste the ribs evenly with barbecue sauce during the last 45 minutes of cooking time.

7. Remove from the heat, carefully remove the rotisserie forks and slide the rod out, and then set the ribs on a large cutting board. Tent the ribs with aluminum foil and let the meat rest for 5 to 10 minutes.

8. Cut away the twine and cut the racks into individual ribs. Serve.

Kansas City Spareribs

Sauce

1 tablespoon (15 ml) olive oil

2 cloves garlic, minced

1 cup (240 g) ketchup

¾ cup (180 ml) water

⅓ cup (75 g) packed brown sugar

1 tablespoon (7 g) paprika

2 teaspoons mild chili powder

¼ teaspoon cayenne

When it comes to the classic barbecued rib, nothing beats Kansas City style. These ribs are coated in a sweet, sticky, smoky sauce with tender, juicy meat. To rant just a little, fall-off-the-bone tender ribs are not the objective when it comes to cooking ribs. Ribs should be on the bone and if that slides out you are left with a slab of meat that lacks character and you lose the true rib-eating experience. Our recipe produces great, flavorful, stay-on-the-bone ribs even with a gas grill.

1. To make the sauce: Heat the oil in a medium-size saucepan over medium heat and sauté the garlic for 15 seconds, until aromatic. Add the remaining sauce ingredients and simmer for 5 minutes, stirring often. Remove from the heat and let cool to room temperature before using.

2. Prepare the grill for medium heat with indirect cooking. Prepare to produce smoke during the cooking process (see page 22).

3. To make the rub: Combine the rub ingredients in a small bowl and set aside.

4. Place the ribs on a cutting board and pat dry with paper towels. Cut away any excess fat from the ribs. Remove the membrane from the back of the ribs by using a blunt knife to work the membrane away from the bone in one corner. Grab hold of the membrane with a paper towel for a good grip and gently peel away. With a little practice, this becomes an easy process.

Rub

⅓ cup (75 g) packed
brown sugar

2 tablespoons (14 g) paprika

2 teaspoons salt

2 teaspoons mild chili powder

1 teaspoon onion powder

½ teaspoon garlic powder

¼ teaspoon cayenne

2 racks spareribs

Yield: 4 to 6 servings

5. Lay the rib racks meat-side down. Apply a small portion of the rub, just enough to season, to the bone side of the racks. Lay one rack on top of the other, bone side to bone side, to form an even shape. Tie the two racks together with kitchen twine between every other bone. The ribs should be held tightly together. Run the rotisserie rod between the racks and secure with the forks. The fork tines should run through the meat as best as possible. The ribs will move a little as the rotisserie turns. They should not flop around, however. Secure to prevent this. Apply the remaining rub evenly over the outer surface of the ribs. A general rule with rubs is that what sticks is the amount needed.

6. Place the ribs on the grill and set a drip pan underneath. Cook for 3 to 4 hours, or until the ribs reach an internal temperature of 185°F (85°C). Test the temperature in several locations. Baste the ribs several times with the sauce during the last hour of cooking to build up a sticky surface.

7. Remove from the heat, carefully remove the rotisserie forks and slide the rod out, and then set the ribs on a large cutting board. Tent the ribs with aluminum foil and let the meat rest for 5 to 10 minutes. Cut away the twine and cut the racks into individual ribs. Serve.

Carnitas

1 bone-in pork shoulder, skin on, 5 to 5½ pounds (2.3 to 2.5 kg)

Rub

2 tablespoons (36 g) coarse salt

1½ teaspoons onion powder

1¼ teaspoons ground cumin

½ teaspoon sugar

½ teaspoon mild chili powder

½ teaspoon dried oregano

½ teaspoon garlic powder

½ teaspoon freshly ground black pepper

1½ cups (355 ml) beer (ale preferred)

2 limes, quartered

Yield: 10 servings

Our simplified method for making great carnitas puts a skin-on pork shoulder on the rotisserie for a few hours to slow roast to perfection. It is not fried in lard like some recipes call for, but has the crispy, crackling skin and the incredibly tender and flavorful meat. This is one of our favorite dishes hands down, and we have the perfect process for getting it right. One trick we use to achieve the combination of tender and crispy is to put the cooked and shredded meat under the broiler for a few minutes. It is this combination of textures that makes carnitas one of the best pork dishes in the world. Serve with warmed tortillas, guacamole, and pico de gallo.

---

1. Trim away any straggling meat or fat pieces from the pork shoulder. Score the skin in a diagonal pattern. Do not pierce into the meat. This will help the fat render from under the skin, leaving it perfectly crisp.

2. To make the rub: Combine the rub ingredients in a small bowl. Pat the pork shoulder dry with paper towels and apply the rub all over the roast. Be sure to really work the seasonings into the meat everywhere possible.

3. Run a long sword skewer through the center of the roast lengthwise to create a pilot hole; since there is a bone running through the middle, take your time and find the right path for the pilot hole. Run the rotisserie rod through the hole and secure with the forks. This is a large roast and needs to be balanced well, with the skin on the outer edge of the roast.

4. Preheat the grill for medium heat with indirect cooking.

5. Place the roast onto the grill and set a drip pan underneath. Cook for 3½ to 4 hours, or until the thickest part of the roast reaches 185°F (85°C). Begin basting with the beer during the last hour of cooking time and repeat the process every 15 minutes until the roast is done. Adjust the temperature of the grill so the meat is cooked at the same time as the skin becomes crisp and the outer surface of the meat is dark brown. One method for achieving this is to increase the grill heat in the last 20 minutes of cooking. Watch closely so the skin does not burn. The skin should be like a hard shell with little fat underneath.

6. Remove from the heat, carefully remove the rotisserie forks and slide the rod out, and then set the roast on a large cutting board. Tent the roast with foil and let the meat rest for 20 to 30 minutes.

7. If you have any cracklings (crispy skin) to deal with, simply cut it away from the roast and break into bite-size chunks. Set aside. Cut the meat into small pieces. The meat should shred quite easily.

8. Squeeze the juice from the lime quarters onto the pork carnitas and serve, or place on a large foil-lined baking sheet and broil for 5 to 6 minutes to gain that mix of textures, squeezing the lime juice on after it comes out of the oven.

Mexican-Style Pork Leg

Rub

1 large pasilla chile

1 teaspoon vegetable oil

1 onion, cut into large chunks

3 or 4 dried chipotle chiles

4 cloves garlic, finely chopped

Juice of 5 limes

2 tablespoons (14 g) ground cumin

2 teaspoons mild chili powder

2 teaspoons dried Mexican oregano

1 teaspoon freshly ground black pepper

1 teaspoon agave or honey

1 teaspoon salt

This pork leg is marinated in an earthy mixture of chipotle and pasilla chiles, cumin, and chili powder. The meat is then slow roasted on the grill, shredded, and topped with a delicious sauce. It's perfect for tacos, burritos, enchiladas, or simply for those who love pork.

1. To make the rub: Brush the pasilla pepper with a little oil and either char on the stove top (gas range) or on your grill. Once the skin has blistered and darkened, remove from the heat and place in a resealable plastic bag. Let sit for 15 minutes. Remove from the bag and, using a paper towel, take off the charred bits. They should lift right off. It is okay if a little remains on the pepper. Cut off the stem, remove the seeds, roughly chop, and place in a food processor.

2. While the pasilla is steaming in the bag, place the chipotle chiles in a bowl. Pour boiling water over the peppers, enough to submerge them. Cover the bowl and let sit for 15 to 20 minutes. Remove the peppers, cut open, and remove the seeds. Roughly chop and place in the food processor. Add the remaining rub ingredients and blend for 10 seconds. The mixture should still have some texture to it, but not large chunks. Reserve ½ to ⅔ cup (120 to 160 ml) of the mixture. Store in an airtight container in the refrigerator until ready to use. Save the remaining mixture to use as a marinade.

3. Line a baking sheet with aluminum foil and top with a sheet of parchment paper. Place the roast on the baking sheet. Apply some of the rub mixture in the deboned portion of the pork leg. Tie the roast in several locations with kitchen twine, forming a consistent bundle, and apply the remaining rub all over the outer portion of the leg. Cover with plastic wrap and place in the refrigerator for 12 to 24 hours.

4. Prepare the grill for medium to medium-high heat with indirect cooking.

1 deboned pork leg,
8 to 10 pounds (3.6 to 4.5 kg)

2 tablespoons (36 g)
coarse salt

1 tablespoon (15 ml)
vegetable oil

¾ cup (180 ml) chicken or
vegetable broth

Kosher salt to taste

Yield: 14 to 16 servings

5. Remove the pork leg from the refrigerator and season with the coarse salt. Run a long sword skewer through the center of the roast lengthwise to create a pilot hole. Run the rotisserie rod through the hole and secure with the forks. Balance as necessary.

6. Place the pork leg on the preheated grill and set a drip pan underneath. Cook for 4 to 6 hours, until the internal temperature reaches 165°F (74°C).

7. Remove from the heat, carefully remove the rotisserie forks and slide the rod out, and then set the pork on a large cutting board. Tent the roast with aluminum foil and let the meat rest for 20 minutes.

8. While the meat is resting, prepare the sauce. Heat the oil in a large skillet or saucepan. Add the reserved marinade to the pan and cook over medium heat for 4 to 5 minutes, stirring occasionally. Warm the broth in the microwave for 20 to 30 seconds. Add to the pan and stir. Decrease the heat to medium-low, add kosher salt to taste, and let the sauce simmer for 8 minutes. Remove from the heat and cover to keep warm.

9. There are two ways you can serve this dish. Simply carve the pork leg and serve with the sauce on top or pull the meat apart into several large portions. Shred the meat and add to the skillet with the sauce. Toss to coat and warm through if needed.

CHAPTER 4

LAMB

If there is one meat that is specifically built for the rotisserie, it is lamb. Due to the limited availability of lamb, this generally means the leg, which is equally good bone in or boneless. When thinking about putting a lamb leg on a rotisserie, many people seem to believe that boneless is the better choice. In our years of cooking bone-in leg of lamb on the rotisserie, we have yet to find one that could not be threaded onto the rod. The shape and structure of a bone-in leg of lamb mean that there is more meat on one side of the bone than the other, and simply running the rod along the bone makes for a near perfect balance.

Of course, there is a lot that can be done with a boneless leg of lamb, like stuffing it with all sorts of ingredients such as herb fillings or an assortment of cheeses. Typically, running a metal rod through a stuffed roast is going to lead to all the stuffing falling out, but again, the shape and structure here make this an easy operation to perform. A boneless lamb leg has a large meat section and then a wide roll of meat. Cutting pockets into the roast makes room for the stuffing, while running the rod through the large meat portion creates the perfect point to secure it all. Yes, there will be tying involved, but do not worry; it can be done in minutes and you will end up with a phenomenal rotisserie lamb dish.

Greek Leg of Lamb

Marinade

Juice of 3 lemons

1 tablespoon (6 g) grated lemon zest

4 to 6 cloves garlic, minced

3 tablespoons (45 ml) olive oil

2 tablespoons (8 g) chopped fresh oregano

2 tablespoons (20 g) chopped red onion

1 boneless leg of lamb, about 4 pounds (1.8 kg)

1½ tablespoons (27 g) salt

2 teaspoons freshly ground black pepper

Yield: 8 servings

Greek leg of lamb is not only delicious but also a good recipe for the rotisserie beginner. This recipe calls for boneless leg of lamb, which will require tying. However, you can use a bone-in (including the shank) leg of lamb as well. You will have to thread that one a little differently. Also, because the surface area is much larger with a bone-in cut, you need more marinade. Simply double the marinade recipe, adjust the cooking time to suit the increase in size, and you will end up with this perfect lemony, herb-coated Greek leg of lamb.

1. To make the marinade: Combine the marinade ingredients in a bowl and let stand at room temperature for 15 minutes while you prepare the lamb leg.

2. Trim loose meat and fat from the leg of lamb and place in a large resealable plastic bag or nonreactive container. Pour the marinade over the lamb and turn to evenly coat with the marinade. Seal the bag or cover the container and place in the refrigerator for 6 to 12 hours. Turn every 2 to 3 hours to make sure the marinade reaches the meat evenly.

3. Prepare the grill for medium heat with indirect cooking.

4. Remove the lamb from the marinade and reserve the marinade. Lay the lamb on a cutting board and tie with kitchen twine into a tight and secure roast. This will take about five ties. Run a long sword skewer through the center of the lamb lengthwise to create a pilot hole. Run the rotisserie rod through the hole and secure with the forks. Balance as necessary. Season the lamb evenly with the salt and pepper.

5. Place the lamb on the preheated grill and set a drip pan underneath. Make sure the lamb can turn freely. Baste with the reserved marinade after the first 10 minutes of cooking time. Do this a few times for about 10 minutes, and then stop. Discard any remaining marinade. Cook until the lamb reaches an internal temperature of 140°F (60°C) for medium or 150°F (66°C) for medium well, 1½ to 2 hours. The roast will shrink during cooking, so adjust the forks when appropriate.

6. Remove from the heat, carefully remove the rotisserie forks and slide the rod out, and then set the lamb on a large cutting board. Tent the lamb with aluminum foil and let the meat rest for 10 minutes. Cut off the twine, slice, and serve.

INDIAN-STYLE LEG OF LAMB

1 boneless leg of lamb, about 4 pounds (1.8 kg)

2 teaspoons salt

½ teaspoon freshly ground black pepper

Marinade

¾ cup (120 g) finely chopped onion

½ cup (120 g) plain whole-milk yogurt

½ cup (8 g) chopped fresh cilantro leaves

3 cloves garlic, minced

Juice of 2 lemons

1 medium chile, finely chopped

1 tablespoon (15 ml) vegetable oil

2 teaspoons ground cumin

1 teaspoon garam masala

1 teaspoon ground coriander

1 teaspoon grated fresh ginger

¼ teaspoon ground cloves

¼ teaspoon ground cardamom

Yield: 8 servings

Leg of lamb is one of our all-time favorite meats to put on the rotisserie. The one thing we like most about this recipe is the yogurt-based marinade. Yogurt has a mild acidity, which helps transfer flavor and improve tenderness, but the best part is that it forms an incredible crust on the meat as it slow roasts.

1. Cut away any excess fat on the lamb leg, but leave a ¼-inch (6 mm) layer intact. Sprinkle all over with the salt and pepper.

2. To make the marinade: Combine the marinade ingredients in a bowl. Place the lamb in a large resealable plastic bag or nonreactive container and pour the marinade over the top. Make sure that the whole roast is well coated. Seal the bag or cover the container and place in the refrigerator for 12 to 24 hours.

3. Prepare the grill for medium-high heat with indirect cooking.

4. Remove the lamb from the marinade. Keep as much of the marinade in place as possible. With kitchen twine, tie the lamb into a tight and secure roast. Start in the center and work toward the ends. Return any lost marinade to the surface as much as possible. Run a long sword skewer through the center of the roast lengthwise to create a pilot hole. Run the rotisserie rod through the hole and secure with the forks. Balance as necessary.

5. Place on the preheated grill and set a drip pan underneath. Cook for 1½ to 2 hours, or until the lamb reaches an internal temperature of 140°F (60°C) for medium or 150°F (66°C) for medium well. The roast will shrink during cooking, so adjust the forks when appropriate.

6. Remove from the heat, carefully remove the rotisserie forks and slide the rod out, and then set the lamb on a large cutting board. Tent the lamb with aluminum foil and let the meat rest for 15 minutes. Cut off the twine, slice, and serve.

Feta and Spinach-Stuffed Leg of Lamb

Stuffing

1¼ cups (38 g) packed fresh spinach, washed, dried, and chopped

½ cup (75 g) crumbled feta cheese

1 small shallot, finely chopped

4 or 5 fresh mint leaves, chopped

1 tablespoon (15 ml) olive oil

1 tablespoon (15 ml) red wine vinegar

⅛ teaspoon salt

⅛ teaspoon freshly ground black pepper

Rub

2 teaspoons salt

1 teaspoon onion powder

½ teaspoon dried oregano

½ teaspoon garlic powder

½ teaspoon freshly ground black pepper

1 boneless leg of lamb, 4 to 4½ pounds (1.8 to 2 kg)

Yield: 8 servings

This butterflied leg of lamb is stuffed with a feta and spinach mixture, rolled, tied, and placed on the rotisserie. You're probably wondering how the filling doesn't fall out during cooking. Well, there are tricks to stuffing a roast for this method of cooking. Follow the instructions exactly for the best results.

1. To make the stuffing: Combine all the stuffing ingredients in a large bowl. Set aside while you prepare the lamb. Cover and place in the refrigerator if it will be more than 30 minutes.

2. To make the rub: Combine all the rub ingredients in a small bowl

3. A boneless leg of lamb is only partially butterflied. To complete the process, open the cut side of the lamb where the bone was removed. With a sharp knife, continue cutting until the leg of lamb can be laid out flat. Make sure the roast remains a single unit. There will be a large, thick section of lamb and a wide flap of meat about 1 to 2 inches (2.5 to 5 cm) thick. Cut slits into the flap for the stuffing; do not cut through the meat.

4. Apply the stuffing to the inside of the meat in an even layer, working the stuffing into the slits. Roll up the butterflied leg of lamb, placing the thickest part in the center. Tie the lamb tightly with kitchen twine, starting at the ends and working toward the center. Replace any stuffing that has fallen out. Apply the rub evenly all over the meat.

5. Run a long sword skewer through the center of the roast lengthwise to create a pilot hole. Avoid the stuffing and go through the large section of meat in the center of the roast. Run the rotisserie rod through the hole and secure with the forks. Balance as necessary.

6. Preheat the grill for medium to medium-high heat with indirect cooking.

7. Place on the preheated grill and set a drip pan underneath. Cook for 60 to 80 minutes, or until the lamb reaches an internal temperature of 140°F (60°C) for medium or 150°F (66°C) for medium well. The lamb will shrink during cooking, so adjust the forks when appropriate.

8. Once cooked, carefully remove the rotisserie forks and rod. Tent the lamb with aluminum foil and let the meat rest for 10 minutes. Cut off the twine and carefully carve the lamb.

Moroccan Leg of Lamb

Rub

1 tablespoon (6 g) cumin seeds

2 teaspoons caraway seeds

2 teaspoons black peppercorns

1¼ tablespoons (23 g) kosher salt

2 teaspoons ground turmeric

4 or 5 cloves garlic, minced

1 tablespoon (15 ml) vegetable oil

2 teaspoons white wine vinegar

1 teaspoon chopped fresh thyme

1 boneless leg of lamb, 4 to 4½ pounds (1.8 to 2 kg)

Yield: 8 servings

This incredibly flavorful rotisserie lamb is coated in fragrant, earthy spices, including cumin, caraway, turmeric, and black pepper. The spices are toasted to add a much deeper level of flavor. This North African–inspired recipe is fantastic served with bulgur wheat, couscous, or even lemony potatoes.

1. To make the rub: Toast the cumin seeds, caraway seeds, and peppercorns in a small, dry skillet over medium heat until they just become fragrant, 1 to 2 minutes. Be sure to shake the pan so the spices do not burn. Once the aromas have blossomed, remove from the heat, transfer to a spice grinder (or coffee grinder), and pulverize. Transfer to a bowl and add the remaining rub ingredients. Stir to combine, forming into a paste. Set aside.

2. Remove any excess fat and loose pieces from the lamb leg. Do not try to remove all the fat, but just some of the thicker pieces and stragglers on the surface. Coat the lamb evenly with the rub and place in a large glass baking dish or large resealable bag. Cover with plastic wrap or seal the bag and place in the refrigerator for 2 to 4 hours.

3. Prepare the grill for medium-high heat with indirect cooking.

4. Remove the lamb from the marinade. Tie the lamb with kitchen twine tightly in several locations. It will take five or six ties. Run a long sword skewer through the center of the roast lengthwise to create a pilot hole. Run the rotisserie rod through the hole and secure with the forks. Balance as necessary.

5. Place the lamb on the preheated grill and set a drip pan underneath. Cook for 60 to 80 minutes, or until the lamb reaches an internal temperature of 140°F (60°C) for medium or 150°F (66°C) for medium well. The roast will shrink during cooking, so adjust the forks when appropriate.

6. Remove from the heat, carefully remove the rotisserie forks and slide the rod out, and then set the lamb on a large cutting board. Tent the roast with aluminum foil and let the meat rest for 10 to 15 minutes. Cut off the twine, slice, and serve.

Spicy Chili and Brown Sugar Lamb

1 boneless leg of lamb (partial bone-in is fine), 4 to 5 pounds (1.8 to 2.3 kg)

Rub

¼ cup (60 g) packed brown sugar

1 tablespoon (18 g) coarse salt

2 teaspoons smoked paprika

1½ to 2 teaspoons spicy chili powder or cayenne

2 teaspoons onion powder

1 teaspoon garlic powder

1 teaspoon freshly ground black pepper

½ teaspoon ground cloves

⅛ teaspoon ground cinnamon

1 recipe Easy Barbecue Sauce (page 63), for serving (optional)

Yield: 6 to 8 servings

Let's face it: Lamb is not at the top of the list of meat choices when it comes to barbecue. The usual suspects are beef brisket, pork butt, and, of course, chicken. However, this recipe defies that concept and uses a spicy barbecue rub on a boneless leg of lamb. You can add a bit of smoke to this recipe as well.

1. Trim off the excess fat and any loose hanging pieces from the lamb. With kitchen twine, tie the roast into a uniform and solid roast. It will take four to five ties to hold it together properly. Run a long sword skewer through the center of the roast lengthwise to create a pilot hole. Run the rotisserie rod through the hole and secure with the forks. Balance as necessary.

2. To make the rub: Combine the rub ingredients in a small bowl and apply evenly to the lamb. Make sure you get as much of the rub on the meat as possible.

3. Prepare the grill for medium heat with indirect cooking. Prepare to produce smoke during the cooking process (see page 22).

4. Place the lamb on the preheated grill and set a drip pan underneath. Cook the lamb for 70 to 90 minutes, until the lamb reaches an internal temperature of 140°F (60°C) for medium or 150°F (66°C) for medium well. The lamb will shrink during cooking, so adjust the forks when appropriate.

5. Remove from the heat, carefully remove the rotisserie forks and slide the rod out, and then set the lamb on a large cutting board. Tent the roast with aluminum foil and let the meat rest for 10 to 12 minutes. Cut off the twine and carve. Serve as is or with barbecue sauce.

MUSTARD-HERB RACK OF LAMB

2 trimmed racks of lamb,
2 to 2½ pounds
(910 to 1,134 g) each

Rub

⅓ cup (60 g) Dijon mustard

4 cloves garlic, minced

1 tablespoon (4 g)
chopped fresh oregano

2½ teaspoons kosher salt

2 teaspoons chopped
fresh thyme

2 teaspoons olive oil

1 teaspoon freshly
ground black pepper

Yield: 4 to 6 servings

Dijon mustard and lamb go really well together. The wet rub for these racks of lamb provides a dramatic enhancement to this recipe. For one, the mustard holds all the seasonings in place to create a flavorful crust. And two, the mustard itself adds a nice bit of tartness, which marries well with the underlying gaminess of the lamb. Do not worry about the mustard being overpowering. As it cooks, the mustard mellows, leaving behind all the savory flavors.

1. Trim off the excess fat and any hanging pieces of meat from the lamb racks. Typically there is a large fat cap on the outside of the rack. Trim this down to no more than ¼ inch (6 mm) in thickness.

2. To make the rub: Combine the rub ingredients in a small bowl. Apply to both racks, and tent the racks with plastic wrap. Allow to sit at room temperature for 20 minutes.

3. Prepare the grill for medium-high heat with indirect cooking.

4. Remove the plastic from the racks and place one rack on top of the other so the bone ends line up. Lace the bones together and, with kitchen twine, tie both racks tightly together in several locations through the bones. Run the rotisserie rod between the racks in a balanced position and secure tightly with the rotisserie forks. Wrap the bone ends in aluminum foil and secure with kitchen twine tied perpendicular to the bones. This will prevent the bone ends from burning.

5. Place the lamb on the preheated grill and set a drip pan underneath. Cook until the center of each rack reaches 145°F (63°C). Measure the internal temperature in the center of the thickest part of the meat section, away from the bone and rotisserie rod. This should take about 1 hour.

6. Remove from the grill, carefully remove the rotisserie forks and slide the rod out, and then set the racks on a large cutting board. Tent the racks with foil and let the meat rest for 10 minutes. Cut away the twine, slice between each bone into individual chops, and serve.

GARLIC-CRUSTED RACK OF LAMB

Crust

¼ cup (60 ml) olive oil

6 cloves garlic, minced

2 tablespoons (8 g) finely chopped fresh oregano

1 tablespoon (2.5 g) chopped fresh thyme

1 tablespoon (18 g) kosher salt

1 teaspoon coarsely ground black pepper

2 trimmed racks of lamb, about 2 to 2½ pounds (910 to 1,134 g) each

Yield: 4 to 6 servings

We love a good rack of lamb. The best part is a flavorful crust around the outer edge of the meat. Since the rack will be sliced for serving and each bit will only hold a small portion of the crust, this can be a potent flavor profile. We have many rack of lamb recipes in our recipe box, but this one has the perfect combination of garlic and fresh herbs that serves lamb so well.

1. To make the crust: Combine the crust ingredients in a bowl and set aside.

2. Prepare the grill for medium-high heat with indirect cooking.

3. Place one rack on top of the other so the bone ends line up. Lace the bones together and, with kitchen twine, tie both racks tightly together in several locations through the bones. Run the rotisserie rod between the racks in a balanced position and secure tightly with the rotisserie forks. Wrap the bone ends in foil and secure with kitchen twine tied perpendicular to the bones. This will prevent the bone ends from burning. Generously apply the crust to the meat portion of the lamb. Avoid getting any of the seasoning onto the bones as this will burn while on the grill.

4. Place the lamb on the preheated grill and set a drip pan underneath. Cook until the center of each rack reaches 145°F (63°C). Measure the internal temperature in the center of the thickest part of the meat section, away from the bone and rotisserie rod. This should take about 1 hour.

5. Remove from the grill, carefully remove the rotisserie forks and slide the rod out, and then set the lamb on a large cutting board. Tent the racks with aluminum foil and let the meat rest for 10 to 12 minutes. Cut away the twine, slice between each bone into individual chops, and serve.

Owensboro Mutton Barbecue

Barbecue Dip

1 cup (235 ml) water

¼ cup (60 ml) Worcestershire sauce

¼ cup (60 ml) apple cider vinegar

1 tablespoon (6 g) freshly ground black pepper

1 tablespoon (15 g) packed brown sugar

1 tablespoon (15 ml) freshly squeezed lemon juice

1 tablespoon (18 g) salt

½ teaspoon ground allspice

Baste

1 cup (235 ml) apple cider vinegar

½ cup (120 ml) Worcestershire sauce

¼ cup (60 ml) freshly squeezed lemon juice

2 tablespoons (12 g) freshly ground black pepper

1 tablespoon (18 g) salt

1 mutton roast (shoulder or leg), 5 pounds (2.3 kg)

Yield: 8 to 10 servings

These days, everyone know about Texas barbecue brisket, Carolina pulled pork, and Kansas City ribs, but few know anything about one of the oldest barbecue traditions in the United States. Deep in the mountains of Kentucky, barbecue means lamb, or, more precisely, mutton. Here, large mutton roasts are slow smoked and served with a completely unique black pepper barbecue sauce. Our rotisserie method may not be completely authentic, but it still turns out some of the best Owensboro barbecue you will come across. Mutton may not be easy to find, so it can be substituted with an equal size lamb roast. This can be served as a sandwich or as is. It is sometimes served with white rice.

---

1. To make the barbecue dip: Combine the dip ingredients in a jar. Cover with a lid and refrigerate, shaking periodically. Warm the dip in the microwave just before serving.

2. To make the baste: Combine the baste ingredients in a small bowl and set aside.

3. Prepare the grill for medium heat with indirect cooking. Prepare to produce smoke during the cooking process (see page 22). This is traditional barbecue and a smoky flavor is part of the recipe.

4. Using kitchen twine, tie the mutton roast into a uniform shape. Run a long sword skewer through the center of the roast lengthwise to create a pilot hole. Run the rotisserie rod through the hole and secure with the forks. Balance as necessary.

5. Place the roast on the preheated grill and set a drip pan underneath. Cook for 4 to 5 hours, applying the baste mixture every 30 minutes, until the roast reaches an internal temperature of 185°F (85°C). The roast will shrink during cooking, so adjust the forks when appropriate.

6. Remove from the heat, carefully remove the rotisserie forks and slide the rod out, and then set the roast on a large cutting board. Tent the roast with aluminum foil and let the meat rest for 20 minutes.

7. Shred or carve the mutton into small pieces. Serve with the warmed barbecue dip on the side.

RED WINE–SWEET ONION LAMB SHOULDER

Marinade

1 medium-size sweet onion

1 tablespoon (15 ml) olive oil

4 to 6 cloves garlic, minced

1 (750 ml) bottle Pinot Noir

2 sprigs fresh thyme

1 sprig fresh rosemary

½ teaspoon sweet paprika

¼ teaspoon ground cloves

¼ teaspoon salt

1 lamb shoulder (or boneless lamb leg), 4 to 4½ pounds (1.8 to 2 kg)

2¼ teaspoons salt

1 teaspoon freshly ground black pepper

Yield: 6 to 8 servings

This lamb shoulder is delicious and succulent. If you can't find lamb shoulder, use a boneless or partial bone-in lamb leg. Serve with mashed potatoes and use the leftovers in stews, soups, and sandwiches.

1. To make the marinade: Grate the sweet onion and place in the center of a clean kitchen cloth. Roll up the cloth and wring out the excess liquid. Meanwhile, heat the olive oil in a large skillet over medium heat. Add the grated onion and cook for 2 minutes. Add the garlic and cook for 30 seconds. Slowly add the Pinot Noir, stirring often. Bring to a simmer and add the remaining marinade ingredients. Decrease the heat to low and simmer the mixture for 10 to 12 minutes, stirring occasionally. Remove from the heat and cool completely. Remove the thyme and rosemary sprigs and divide the mixture into two portions. Reserve half as a baste, storing it in a tightly covered jar in the refrigerator.

2. Cut off excess fat from the lamb. Pat dry with paper towels and place in a large resealable plastic bag or a glass baking dish. Pour the remaining marinade over the meat and turn meat to coat. Seal the bag or cover the dish with plastic wrap. Refrigerate for 6 to 24 hours.

3. Prepare the grill for medium-high heat with indirect cooking.

4. Remove the lamb from the bag, discarding the marinade. Blot the lamb lightly with paper towels to remove excess moisture. Run a long sword skewer through the center of the roast lengthwise to create a pilot hole. Run the rotisserie rod through the hole and secure with the forks. If using a boneless lamb leg, tie the roast with kitchen twine. Season the meat with salt and pepper.

5. Place the lamb on the preheated grill and set a drip pan underneath. Cook for 75 to 90 minutes, or until the internal temperature at the thickest point reaches 145°F (63°C). Reheat the reserved marinade in the microwave for 20 seconds. Begin basting after the first 20 minutes of cooking. Repeat every 10 minutes until the roast is almost done. Adjust the forks when appropriate.

6. Remove from the heat, carefully remove the rotisserie forks and rod, and set the lamb on a large cutting board. Tent the roast with foil and let the meat rest for 15 minutes. Carve into ½-inch (1.3 cm)-thick slices.

LAMB DÖNER KEBAB

Garlic Yogurt Sauce

1 cup (240 g) plain yogurt

3 cloves garlic, minced

1 tablespoon (15 ml) freshly
squeezed lemon juice

½ teaspoon salt

¼ teaspoon freshly
ground black pepper

¼ teaspoon sugar

⅛ teaspoon cayenne pepper

The döner kebab is not a kebab in the modern sense. Derived from ancient origins, this dish was standardized in the mid-twentieth century and gained worldwide popularity. You are probably more familiar with the minced meat version that is sliced and served in gyros. In its original form, this is a stack of thinly sliced meat placed on a rod and cooked vertically in front of a heat source. That meat is typically lamb, but it can be beef or chicken. Today, it is frequently a combination of lamb and beef. As the outer edges cook, they are carved off and served. We have modified this recipe so readers can make it on their backyard grill. We will warn you, though, that this is a more advanced rotisserie dish and is a little labor-intensive. However, the outcome is delicious and it can be dressed up like a gyro or shawarma.

1. To make the garlic yogurt sauce: Combine the sauce ingredients in a nonreactive bowl. Cover with plastic wrap and store in the refrigerator until ready to use. This sauce can be made a day ahead to allow the flavors to really mesh together.

2. To make the marinade: Combine the marinade ingredients in a small bowl.

3. Cut the lamb into uniform ⅓- to ½-inch (8 to 13 mm) round slices. It is important that they be the same size. Cut smaller slices thicker and pound with a mallet to match the size of the other slices. Place in a large resealable plastic bag and pour the marinade over the meat. Make sure all the slices are well coated. Release air from the bag, seal, and place in the refrigerator for 12 to 24 hours.

4. Prepare the grill for medium to medium-high heat with indirect cooking.

Marinade

¼ cup (60 ml) olive oil

Juice of 2 large lemons

2 tablespoons (30 ml) red wine vinegar

3 or 4 cloves garlic, minced

1 tablespoon (18 g) kosher salt

2 teaspoons onion powder

1 teaspoon freshly ground black pepper

1 teaspoon dried oregano

¼ teaspoon ground cardamom

¼ teaspoon ground turmeric

¼ teaspoon ground allspice

¼ teaspoon paprika

1 boneless leg of lamb, about 4 pounds (1.8 kg)

6 to 8 soft pitas or flatbread

2 large tomatoes, sliced

1 white onion, thinly sliced

Yield: 6 to 8 servings

5. Remove the meat slices from the marinade and stack into a uniform tower. Use 6 or more bamboo skewers to secure the tower. Fold any dangling pieces into the tower and secure. Once all the meat is stacked and stable, run a long sword skewer through the center of the stack lengthwise to create a pilot hole. Run the rotisserie rod through the hole and secure with the forks. Rotate the rod to make sure that this is entirely secure and turns evenly. Balance as necessary. If you have a counterbalance, use that to adjust the balance.

6. Place the stack on the preheated grill and set a drip pan underneath. The cooking time will vary depending on the grill and the heat, but it should be completely cooked within 1 to 1½ hours. It is important to allow this dish to cook through completely without the exterior drying out or burning, so adjust the temperature accordingly. In the traditional method, the cooked exterior is carved away as the "roast" cooks. That would be difficult with this arrangement. Cook until the internal temperature, measured in several locations, reaches a minimum of 140°F (60°C).

7. Remove the meat and rotisserie rod from the grill and without removing the rod, place on a cutting board, cover, and allow to rest for 5 to 10 minutes. Carving from the sides, cut into small pieces, working around the exterior and removing the skewers as you go. You will carve this all the way down to the rod. Toss the small, cut pieces together to mix the crusty exterior sections with the moister center pieces.

8. Serve the meat in warmed pitas with the garlic yogurt sauce and tomato and onion slices.

CHAPTER 5

CHICKEN, TURKEY, AND GAME HENS

We are well aware that the word that usually follows rotisserie is chicken. There is, of course, much more that can be done with poultry, but few things are better than a rotisserie chicken. There are now entire cookbooks filled with recipes that can be made with store-bought rotisserie chickens. This means that many people now consider this type of chicken a convenience food item and not an actual dish to be cooked.

Store-bought rotisserie chicken is fine. It is not, however, terribly flavorful. The problem is that these chickens tend to be on the bland side and generally spend more time sitting on a warming table than on an actual rotisserie. We prefer making our own rotisserie chicken and serving it just 10 minutes after coming off the grill. This approach offers a fresher and much more flavorful rotisserie chicken that is loaded with possibilities. In short, rotisserie chicken should not be the ingredient for other dishes first: It should be the star attraction.

Don't limit rotisserie cooking to just chickens, however. This is also a wonderful method for preparing a holiday turkey—that is, provided the rotisserie motor can handle the weight. Be sure to pick smaller turkeys anywhere from 12 to 14 pounds (5.5 to 6.4 kg) for this type of cooking. With this method, you can both grill and smoke turkeys to perfection without worrying about uneven cooking or drying out. The other advantage of putting the turkey on the rotisserie is that it frees up the oven for all of the side dishes that complete the meal.

Despite the name, Cornish game hens are not game. They are actually chickens specifically bred for their small size. In this case, the expression "tastes like chicken" is exactly true. Game hens are cooked and eaten just like chicken. For the average person, one game hen is a good-size meal, so plan on that and you will have enough for everyone with the potential for leftovers.

DELI-STYLE ROTISSERIE CHICKEN

1 whole chicken, 3 to 3½ pounds (1.4 to 1.6 kg)

Rub

1½ teaspoons salt

½ teaspoon onion powder

½ teaspoon paprika

¼ teaspoon mustard powder

¼ teaspoon garlic powder

¼ teaspoon freshly ground black pepper

¼ teaspoon mild chili powder

1 large onion, peeled and left whole (for cavity)

Yield: 4 servings

Every year, millions of chickens get thrown into giant rotisserie ovens with a sprinkling of seasoning, then placed into little plastic, bubble-top boxes to be taken home and turned into soups, sandwiches, or enchiladas. The problem is that these are not the best chickens, as they lack flavor and may have been sitting on a warming table for hours. You can do better than that. Cook your own deli-style rotisserie chicken in less than two hours and have a delicious meal, no matter how it is served.

1. Prepare the grill for high heat with indirect cooking.

2. Pat the chicken dry inside and out with paper towels.

3. To make the rub: Combine the rub ingredients in a small bowl and apply all over the chicken. Get the seasonings under the skin of the breast as well. Truss the chicken with kitchen twine. Run the rotisserie rod through the onion and insert it into the chicken cavity. Use a paring knife to cut a pilot hole in the onion to make this easier. Continue to run the rod through the chicken and secure with the rotisserie forks.

4. Place on the preheated grill with a drip pan underneath. Cook for about 1 hour, or until the meat in the thighs and legs reaches 175°F (80°C). The breasts should be 165°F (74°C).

5. Remove from the heat, carefully remove the rotisserie forks and slide the rod and onion out, and then set the chicken on a large cutting board. Tent the chicken with aluminum foil and let it rest for 15 to 20 minutes before cutting off the twine and carving.

Tangerine-Tarragon Chicken

Marinade

½ cup (120 ml) freshly squeezed tangerine juice

¼ cup (60 ml) freshly squeezed lime juice

3 cloves garlic, minced

2 tablespoons (30 ml) olive oil

1½ tablespoons (23 g) packed brown sugar

1½ tablespoons (6 g) chopped fresh tarragon

1½ teaspoons salt

1 teaspoon grated fresh ginger

½ teaspoon white pepper

1 whole chicken, 3 to 3½ pounds (1.4 to 1.6 kg)

Yield: 4 servings

We love rotisserie chicken. We love it so much that we have a box full of great recipes. With this one, we combine the fruity flavor of tangerine with the licorice flavor of tarragon. There is a slightly sweet note to this rotisserie chicken, but it is not what stands out. As the tangerine in the marinade cooks, the sweetness fades and the citrus pops out. What you get is a savory and delicious chicken that is so much better than any store can make.

1. To make the marinade: Combine the marinade ingredients in a small bowl and set aside.

2. Pat the chicken dry inside and out with paper towels. Cut off any extra, straggling skin. Place the chicken in a large resealable plastic bag or nonreactive container. Add the marinade, making sure the bird is well coated. Seal the bag or cover the container and place in the refrigerator for 3 to 4 hours.

3. Prepare the grill for medium-high heat with indirect cooking.

4. Remove the chicken from the bag and pour the marinade into a saucepan. Bring to a quick boil over high heat, decrease the heat to medium, and simmer for 3 minutes. Remove from the heat and let cool.

5. Truss the chicken with kitchen twine, run the rotisserie rod through the cavity, and secure with the rotisserie forks. Place on the preheated grill, set a drip pan underneath, and pour 1 cup (235 ml) hot water into the pan. Cook for 1 to 1½ hours, or until the meat in the thighs and legs reaches 175°F (80°C). The breasts should be 165°F (74°C). Baste the chicken after the first 20 minutes of cooking time with the reserved marinade and stop basting about 10 minutes before the chicken is done.

6. Remove from the heat, carefully remove the rotisserie forks and slide the rod out, and then set the chicken on a large cutting board. Tent the chicken with aluminum foil and let it rest for 10 to 12 minutes before cutting off the twine and carving.

Buffalo Chicken

1 whole chicken,
3 to 3½ pounds (1.4 to 1.6 kg)

Basic Brine (page 50)

Sauce

1 teaspoon olive oil

2 cloves garlic, minced

½ cup (1 stick, 112 g) unsalted
butter, cubed

⅔ cup (160 ml) hot sauce

1 tablespoon (15 ml) freshly
squeezed lemon juice

1 teaspoon
Worcestershire sauce

½ teaspoon salt

¼ teaspoon cayenne
(optional)

¼ teaspoon freshly
ground black pepper

Yield: 4 servings

Who doesn't love a nice plate of Buffalo wings? Well, we've adapted the recipe to include a whole rotisserie chicken. This way you have more than just the wing and rather an actual meal. Serve this dish with a creamy potato salad. It's a perfect summer dish for the whole family to enjoy.

1. Brine the chicken for 4 to 6 hours in a large resealable plastic bag or a plastic or glass container in the refrigerator. Make sure the chicken is completely submerged in the brine.

2. Prepare the sauce during the last half hour of brine time: Heat the oil in a saucepan over medium heat and add the garlic. Cook for no more than 30 seconds. Add all the remaining ingredients and simmer for 3 to 4 minutes, until the butter has melted through and the sauce is well combined. Remove from the heat and keep warm until ready to use.

3. Prepare the grill for medium-high heat with indirect cooking.

4. Remove the chicken from the brine. Give it a quick rinse and pat dry inside and out with paper towels. Truss the chicken with kitchen twine, run the rotisserie rod through the chicken, and secure with the rotisserie forks.

5. Place the chicken on the preheated grill and cook for 60 to 80 minutes, basting with sauce after the first 30 minutes of cooking time. Do this several times, until the chicken is nearly done. Cook until the meat in the thighs and legs reaches 175°F (80°C). The breasts should be 165°F (74°C).

6. Remove from the heat, carefully remove the rotisserie forks and slide the rod out, and then set the chicken on a large cutting board. Tent the chicken with aluminum foil and let it rest for 10 minutes before cutting off the twine and carving.

7. If you leave the chicken on until it reaches 185°F (85°C) in the thighs and legs, you should be able to shred it. Just make a double batch of sauce and save half of it for later. Once the chicken is shredded, add some of the reserved sauce, toss to coat, and serve in sandwiches.

PERUVIAN CHICKEN

Marinade

¼ cup (60 ml) white vinegar

¼ cup (60 ml) dry white wine

2 tablespoons (30 ml) olive oil

3 or 4 cloves garlic, minced

1 tablespoon (7 g) sweet paprika

1 tablespoon (7 g) ground cumin

1 teaspoon freshly ground black pepper

1¼ teaspoons salt

1 whole chicken, 3½ to 4 pounds (1.6 to 1.8 kg)

Yield: 4 servings

This deliciously spiced Peruvian-style chicken gets its gorgeous color from the paprika. Known also as Super Chicken or El Pollo Loco, this rotisserie version of a popular recipe is truly divine. We recommend serving any spiced chicken with mild side dishes, such as plain rice, steamed vegetables, or salad greens.

1. To make the marinade: Combine the marinade ingredients in a bowl and set aside.

2. Cut off any dangling skin from the chicken and pat dry inside and out with paper towels. Place in a large resealable plastic bag or nonreactive bowl. Pour the marinade over the chicken and, using tongs, turn the chicken a few times to coat well. Seal the bag or cover the bowl tightly with plastic wrap and place in the refrigerator for 6 to 8 hours.

3. Prepare the grill for medium-high heat with indirect cooking.

4. Truss the chicken with kitchen twine. Run the rotisserie rod through the chicken and secure with the forks. If any remaining marinade is left in the bag or bowl, brush it onto the chicken.

5. Place the chicken on the preheated grill and set a drip pan underneath. Cook for 70 to 90 minutes, or until the internal temperature of the thigh reaches at least 175°F (80°C). The breast meat should be 165°F (74°C).

6. Remove from the heat, carefully remove the rotisserie forks and slide the rod out, and then set the chicken on a large cutting board. Tent the chicken with aluminum foil and let it rest for 10 minutes before cutting off the twine and carving.

THREE PEPPER CHICKEN

1 whole chicken,
3 to 3½ pounds (1.4 to 1.6 kg)

Basic Brine (page 50)

Rub

3 tablespoons (42 g) unsalted
butter, at room temperature

2 tablespoons (30 ml) freshly
squeezed orange juice

1 teaspoon orange zest

2 cloves garlic, minced

1 teaspoon lemon pepper

½ teaspoon white pepper

½ teaspoon cayenne

Yield: 4 servings

Brined and rubbed with three types of pepper and, of course, butter, this rotisserie chicken is simple and flavorful. The whole chicken is the perfect Sunday dinner, or cut it up and add to sandwiches, soups, and enchiladas. In fact, this is the perfect "start with rotisserie chicken" ingredient for most any recipe.

1. Brine the chicken for 2 to 4 hours in a large resealable plastic bag or a plastic or glass container in the refrigerator. Make sure the chicken is completely submerged in the brine. Remove the chicken from the brine. Give it a quick rinse and pat dry inside and out with paper towels.

2. Preheat the grill for medium-high heat with indirect cooking.

3. To make the rub: In a small bowl, combine the softened butter and orange juice. Add the remaining rub ingredients and stir until completely combined.

4. Apply the rub mixture all over the chicken and under the skin of the breast. To get the rub under the skin, gently lift it away from the meat with your fingers and push the rub as far under the skin as possible. Truss the chicken with kitchen twine. Run the rotisserie rod through the chicken and tightly secure with the rotisserie forks.

5. Place the chicken on the preheated grill and set a drip pan underneath. Cook for 60 to 80 minutes, or until the internal temperature of the thigh reaches 175°F to 180°F (80°C to 82°C) and the breast is 165°F to 170°F (74°C to 77°C).

6. Remove from the heat, carefully remove the rotisserie forks and slide the rod out, and then set the chicken on a large cutting board. Tent the chicken with aluminum foil and let it rest for 10 to 15 minutes before cutting off the twine and carving.

LEMON HERB CHICKEN

1 whole chicken, 3 to 4 pounds (1.4 to 1.8 kg)

Basic Brine (page 50)

1 lemon (for cavity)

Rub

2 tablespoons (30 ml) olive oil

1 tablespoon (15 ml) freshly squeezed lemon juice

1 or 2 cloves garlic, minced

1 teaspoon lemon zest

½ teaspoon finely chopped fresh rosemary

½ teaspoon finely chopped fresh marjoram

½ teaspoon finely chopped fresh thyme

¼ teaspoon dried savory

¼ teaspoon dried basil

¼ teaspoon freshly ground black pepper

Baste

2 tablespoons (30 ml) freshly squeezed lemon juice

2 tablespoons (30 ml) white wine

1 tablespoon (15 ml) olive oil

1½ teaspoons rub mixture

1 teaspoon honey

¼ teaspoon mild chili powder

Yield: 4 servings

There are a lot of ways to cook a whole chicken, and we have tried them all. What we have found time and time again is that the best method is the rotisserie. What we have created here is the triple threat chicken that is brined, rubbed, and basted to achieve maximum flavor and tenderness. It might sound complicated, but this recipe is nearly as easy as going to the store.

1. Brine the chicken for 4 hours in a large resealable plastic bag or a plastic or glass container in the refrigerator. Make sure the chicken is completely submerged in the brine. Remove the chicken from the brine. Give it a quick rinse and pat dry inside and out with paper towels.

2. Prepare the grill for medium-high heat with indirect cooking.

3. To make the rub: Combine the rub ingredients in a small bowl. Reserve 1½ teaspoons for the baste. Apply the remaining rub all over the chicken, particularly under the skin of the breast and inside the cavity. To get the rub under the skin, gently work a finger between the meat and the skin. It will pull away. Be careful not to tear it.

4. To make the baste: Combine all the baste ingredients in a bowl.

5. Truss the chicken with kitchen twine. Run the rotisserie rod through the lemon and insert it into the chicken cavity. Use a paring knife to cut a pilot hole in the lemon to make this easier. Continue to run the rod through the chicken and secure with the rotisserie forks.

6. Place the chicken on the preheated grill, set a drip pan underneath, and add 2 cups (470 ml) hot water to the pan. Begin basting the chicken every 10 minutes until the thigh and leg meat reaches 175°F (80°C) and the breast is 165°F (74°C), 1 to 1½ hours.

7. Remove from the heat, carefully remove the rotisserie forks and slide the rod out, and then set the chicken on a large cutting board. Tent the chicken with aluminum foil and let it rest for 15 to 20 minutes before cutting off the twine and carving.

PANCETTA-STUFFED CHICKEN

1 whole chicken,
3½ to 4 pounds (1.6 to 1.8 kg)

8 to 12 thinly sliced
pancetta rounds

1 teaspoon onion powder

½ teaspoon freshly
ground black pepper

1 lemon

Yield: 4 servings

While the rotisserie bastes what it cooks, this recipe takes that idea to a whole new level. Thin strips of pancetta are stuffed under the skin of the chicken. This means that as the chicken cooks, the pancetta melts and adds flavor and moisture to the meat. If you like bacon-wrapped chicken, this is all that and a whole lot more.

1. Preheat the grill for medium-high heat with indirect cooking.

2. Rinse the chicken under cold water and pat dry inside and out with paper towels. With your fingers, lift away the skin from the chicken breasts and work around the legs, lifting the skin as you go. Don't tear the skin, but separate as much as possible from the meat. Now work the pancetta slices under the skin and over the meat, distributing it as evenly as possible. Avoid clumps of pancetta. Season with the onion powder and pepper. Truss the chicken with kitchen twine. Run the rotisserie rod through the lemon and insert it into the chicken cavity. Use a paring knife to cut a pilot hole in the lemon to make this easier. Continue to run the rod through the chicken and secure with the rotisserie forks.

3. Place the chicken on the preheated grill, set a drip pan underneath, and add 2 cups (470 ml) hot water to the pan. Cook for 1 to 1½ hours, or until the meat in the thighs and legs reaches 175°F (80°C). The breasts should be 165°F (74°C).

4. Remove from the heat, carefully remove the rotisserie forks and slide the rod out, and then set the chicken on a large cutting board. Tent the chicken with aluminum foil and let it rest for 10 to 15 minutes before cutting off the twine and carving.

Huli Huli Chicken (*Hawaiian Chicken*)

Sauce

Juice of 4 large limes

½ cup (120 ml) soy sauce

¼ cup (80 g) honey

3 tablespoons (45 g) ketchup

3 tablespoons (45 g) packed dark brown sugar

2 cloves garlic, minced

1½ teaspoons sesame oil

¼ teaspoon freshly ground black pepper

¼ teaspoon red pepper flakes

1 whole chicken, 3 to 3½ pounds (1.4 to 1.6 kg)

¼ teaspoon salt

¼ teaspoon freshly ground black pepper

1 large onion, peeled but left whole (for cavity)

Yield: 4 servings

Huli *means "turned" in Hawaiian, and this is one of our favorite rotisserie chicken dishes. We use a teriyaki-style glaze as both a marinade and a baste to build a strong layering of flavors. This has always been one of our most popular recipes and since the marinating time is only an hour, it can be prepared quickly and easily.*

1. To make the sauce: Combine the sauce ingredients in a medium-size bowl. Divide the mixture into two portions. Reserve half of the mixture for basting and use half for the marinade.

2. Place the chicken in a large resealable plastic bag or nonreactive bowl and pour the marinade over the top. With tongs, turn the chicken to coat. Seal the bag or cover the bowl and place in the refrigerator for 1 to 2 hours.

3. Prepare the grill for medium-high heat with indirect cooking.

4. Remove the chicken from the bag, discarding the marinade. Pat dry with paper towels inside and out and season with the salt and pepper. Truss the chicken with kitchen twine. Run the rotisserie rod through the onion and insert it into the chicken cavity. Use a paring knife to cut a pilot hole in the onion to make this easier. Continue to run the rod through the chicken and secure with the rotisserie forks.

5. Place the chicken on the preheated grill, set a drip pan underneath, and cook for 1 to 1½ hours, or until the meat in the thighs and legs reaches 175°F (80°C). The breasts should be 165°F (74°C). Begin basing the chicken with the reserved sauce during the last 30 minutes of cooking time.

6. Remove from the heat, carefully remove the rotisserie forks and slide the rod out, and then set the chicken on a large cutting board. Tent the chicken with aluminum foil and let it rest for 15 to 20 minutes before cutting off the twine and carving.

Traditional French Chicken

1 whole chicken,
3½ to 4 pounds (1.6 to 1.8 kg)

Basic Brine (page 50)

Rub

3 tablespoons (42 g) unsalted
butter, at room temperature

2 or 3 cloves garlic, minced

2 teaspoons chopped
fresh rosemary

2 teaspoons chopped
fresh thyme

¼ teaspoon freshly ground
black pepper

Baste

½ cup (120 ml) chicken
stock, warmed

⅓ cup (80 ml) dry white wine

1 tablespoon (15 ml) olive oil

Yield: 4 servings

This is a traditional French-style chicken that uses butter, garlic, and herbs. The only difference is that this bird is brined first. The chicken is perfect for drip pan vegetables such as carrots or potatoes. It will also produce a delicious gravy, so be sure to use these drippings wisely.

---

1. Brine the chicken for 2 to 4 hours in a large resealable plastic bag or a plastic or glass container in the refrigerator. Make sure the chicken is completely submerged in the brine.

2. Prepare the grill for medium-high heat with indirect cooking.

3. Remove the chicken from the brine. Give it a quick rinse (do not over rinse) and pat dry inside and out with paper towels. Truss the chicken with kitchen twine. Run the rotisserie rod through the chicken and secure with the rotisserie forks.

4. To make the rub: Combine the rub ingredients in a bowl and apply all over the chicken. Do not forget to get some of it under the breast skin and inside the body cavity.

5. To make the baste: Combine the baste ingredients in a small bowl.

6. Place the chicken on the preheated grill, set a drip pan underneath, and add 1 to 2 cups (235 to 470 ml) hot water to the pan. If you intend to make a gravy, make sure that the drip pan does not run dry. Cook the chicken, applying the baste several times after the first 30 minutes of cooking, for 80 to 90 minutes, or until the meat in the thighs and legs reaches 175°F (80°C). The breasts should be 165°F (74°C).

7. Remove from the heat, carefully remove the rotisserie forks and slide the rod out, and then set the chicken on a large cutting board. Tent the chicken with aluminum foil and let it rest for 15 minutes before cutting off the twine and carving.

Oregano Chicken

Rub

⅓ cup (22 g) finely chopped fresh oregano

2 cloves garlic, minced

Zest of 1 lemon

1 tablespoon (15 ml) olive oil

2 teaspoons kosher salt

¼ teaspoon freshly ground black pepper

1 whole chicken, 3 to 3½ pounds (1.4 to 1.6 kg)

Baste

Juice of 1 lemon

1 tablespoon (4 g) chopped fresh oregano

1 tablespoon (15 ml) white wine vinegar

1 teaspoon sugar

¼ teaspoon salt

1 lemon (for cavity)

Yield: 4 servings

Back in college, there was this little Greek diner where every Thursday's special was oregano chicken. Tart with lemon juice, doused in olive oil, and packed with fresh oregano, it was a weekly treat. This is our take on that recipe. It is lighter, healthier, and even more delicious.

1. To make the rub: Combine the rub ingredients in a small bowl and stir to make a wet paste. Pat the chicken dry with paper towels and apply the rub all over, including under the breast skin. Place the chicken on a large plate, cover with plastic wrap, and place in the refrigerator for 4 hours.

2. To make the baste: Combine all the baste ingredients in a small bowl and set aside.

3. Remove the chicken from the refrigerator and let sit at room temperature for 20 minutes.

4. Prepare the grill for medium-high heat with indirect cooking.

5. Truss the chicken with kitchen twine. Run the rotisserie rod through the lemon and insert it into the chicken cavity. Use a paring knife to cut a pilot hole in the lemon to make this easier. Continue to run the rod through the chicken and secure with the rotisserie forks.

6. Place the chicken on the preheated grill, set a drip pan underneath, and add 1 cup (235 ml) hot water to the pan. Cook the chicken for 1½ hours, applying the baste during the last 30 minutes of cooking time, until the meat in the thighs and legs reaches 175°F (80°C). The breasts should be 165°F (74°C).

7. Remove from the heat, carefully remove the rotisserie forks and slide the rod out, and then set the chicken on a large cutting board. Tent the chicken with aluminum foil and let it rest for 15 to 20 minutes before cutting off the twine and carving.

Cherry Cola Barbecued Chicken

Barbecue Sauce

¾ cup (180 g) ketchup

⅔ cup (160 ml) cherry cola

¼ cup (60 ml) apple cider vinegar

2 tablespoons (30 g) packed brown sugar

1 tablespoon (20 g) molasses

¼ teaspoon salt

¼ teaspoon freshly ground black pepper

Rub

2 teaspoons salt

2 teaspoons onion powder

1 teaspoon mustard powder

½ teaspoon freshly ground black pepper

½ teaspoon garlic powder

1 whole chicken, 3 to 4 pounds (1.4 to 1.8 kg)

1 medium-size onion, peeled but whole (for cavity)

Yield: 4 to 6 servings

It is not unusual to add cola to barbecue sauces. In fact, it adds a nice caramel flavor to the finished product. This recipe uses cherry cola, lending a bit of tart fruitiness as well as a good dose of sweetness to the sauce. Double the sauce recipe and serve half of it as a table sauce, along with the carved chicken, if desired. Or shred the chicken, combine with the sauce, and serve in sandwich buns.

---

1. To make the barbecue sauce: Combine all the ingredients in a medium-size saucepan over medium heat and simmer for 5 to 6 minutes, until the mixture is smooth and well blended. Stir often and watch for burning. Remove from the heat and let the sauce cool at least 10 minutes before using.

2. To make the rub: Combine all the rub ingredients in a small bowl.

3. Preheat the grill for medium-high heat with indirect cooking.

4. Pat the chicken dry inside and out with paper towels. Apply the rub all over the bird, under the breast skin, and inside the body cavity.

5. Truss the chicken with kitchen twine. Run the rotisserie rod through the onion and insert it into the chicken cavity. Use a paring knife to cut a pilot hole in the onion to make this easier. Continue to run the rod through the chicken and secure with the rotisserie forks.

6. Place the chicken on the preheated grill and set a drip pan underneath. Cook for 60 to 80 minutes, or until the meat in the thighs and legs reaches 175°F (80°C). The breasts should be 165°F (74°C). Baste the chicken with the barbecue sauce during the last half of the cooking time. Do so every 7 to 10 minutes, until the bird is nearly done and well coated with the sauce.

7. Remove from the heat, carefully remove the rotisserie forks and slide the rod out, and then set the chicken on a large cutting board. Tent the chicken with aluminum foil and let it rest for 10 to 15 minutes before cutting off the twine and carving.

Spanish Paprika Chicken

1 whole chicken,
3 to 3½ pounds (1.4 to 1.6 kg)

Basic Brine (page 50)

Rub

2 tablespoons (30 ml) olive oil

1 tablespoon (7 g)
smoked paprika

1 tablespoon (4 g) finely
chopped fresh oregano

2 cloves garlic, minced

2 teaspoons honey

1 teaspoons white
wine vinegar

½ teaspoon freshly
ground black pepper

Yield: 4 servings

Simple yet elegant, this classic dish is a quick and easy rotisserie chicken that seems like it took hours to make. Of course, we start with a simple brine to ensure that the chicken remains tender and moist. Then it is coated in a flavorful wet rub before hitting the grill. This is one of our favorite rotisserie chicken dishes. Not only is it delicious, but it also makes the best soup you can imagine.

1. Brine the chicken for 4 to 6 hours in a large resealable plastic bag or a plastic or glass container in the refrigerator. Make sure the chicken is completely submerged in the brine. Remove the chicken from the brine. Give it a quick rinse and pat dry inside and out with paper towels.

2. To make the rub: Combine the rub ingredients and apply all over the chicken, making sure to get under the skin of the breast and inside the bird. Truss the chicken, then run the rotisserie rod through the chicken and secure with the rotisserie forks.

3. Prepare the grill for medium-high heat with indirect cooking.

4. Place the chicken on the preheated grill, set a drip pan underneath, and add 1 cup (235 ml) hot water. Cook the chicken for 1 to 1½ hours, or until the meat in the thighs and legs reaches 175°F (80°C). The breasts should be 165°F (74°C).

5. Remove from the heat, carefully remove the rotisserie forks and slide the rod out, and then set the chicken on a large cutting board. Tent the chicken with aluminum foil and let it rest for 15 minutes before cutting off the twine and carving.

Peri Peri Chicken

1 whole chicken,
about 3½ pounds (1.6 kg)

Basic Brine
(page 50, optional)

Rub

1 small shallot, finely chopped

Juice and zest of
1 medium-size lemon

3 tablespoons (42 g) unsalted
butter, at room temperature

2 red chiles, finely sliced

2 cloves garlic, minced

1 tablespoon (4 g)
chopped fresh oregano

2 teaspoons smoked paprika

1¼ teaspoons salt (omit if
brining the chicken)

½ teaspoon freshly ground
black pepper

1 whole onion, peeled but
left whole (optional)

Yield: 4 servings

Peri peri chicken is a hybrid of African and Portuguese cuisines that traditionally call for peri peri (or piri piri) chile peppers. If you happen to find peri peri peppers, use them. If not, use the hot red chiles that can be found at the local grocery store. While preparing this dish, keep in mind your tolerance for spice. If you can handle the heat, then increase the amount of chiles used in the recipe. If not, simply reduce them.

---

1. If brining the chicken, place in a large resealable plastic bag or a plastic or glass container and place in the refrigerator for 4 hours. Make sure the chicken is completely submerged in the brine. Remove the chicken from the brine. Give it a quick rinse and pat dry inside and out with paper towels.

2. To make the rub: Combine the rub ingredients in a small bowl, omitting the salt if you brined the chicken, and apply all over the chicken, under the skin of the breast, and inside the body cavity.

3. Prepare the grill for medium-high with indirect cooking.

4. Truss the chicken with kitchen twine. Run the rotisserie rod through the onion and insert it into the chicken cavity. Use a paring knife to cut a pilot hole in the onion to make this easier. Continue to run the rod through the chicken and secure with the rotisserie forks.

5. Place the chicken on the preheated grill and set a drip pan underneath. Cook the chicken for 70 to 90 minutes, or until the meat in the thighs and legs reaches 175°F (80°C). The breasts should be 165°F (74°C).

6. Remove from the heat, carefully remove the rotisserie forks and slide the rod out, and then set the chicken on a large cutting board. Tent the chicken with aluminum foil and let it rest for 15 minutes before cutting off the twine and carving.

CUBAN MOJO CHICKEN

1 whole chicken,
about 3½ pounds (1.6 kg)

Marinade

½ cup (120 ml) freshly
squeezed orange juice

¼ cup (60 ml) freshly
squeezed lime juice

Zest of 2 limes

1 or 2 chiles, chopped

3 cloves garlic, minced

2 tablespoons (30 ml)
vegetable oil

1 tablespoon (15 ml)
apple cider vinegar

2 teaspoons sugar

1½ teaspoons ground cumin

1¼ teaspoons salt

½ teaspoon dried oregano

½ teaspoon freshly
ground black pepper

Yield: 4 servings

This Cuban-inspired chicken recipe relies heavily on citrus not only to flavor the meat but also to help tenderize it. This recipe also calls for chopped chiles. We recommend red chiles, but you can use something milder like a serrano, mild Hatch, or jalapeño chile. Just remove the seeds before adding the pieces to the marinade. Serve the chicken over plain rice with black beans or over fresh salad greens.

1. Trim off any excess skin from the chicken, pat dry inside and out with paper towels, and place in a deep nonreactive bowl.

2. To make the marinade: Combine the marinade ingredients and reserve half for basting. Pour the remaining half over the chicken, making sure to coat it evenly, inside and out. Cover the bowl with plastic wrap and place in the refrigerator for 4 to 6 hours.

3. Prepare the grill for medium-high heat with indirect cooking.

4. Remove the chicken from the bowl, discard the marinade, pat dry with paper towels, and truss with kitchen twine. Slide the rotisserie rod through the chicken and secure tightly.

5. Place the chicken on the preheated grill, set a drip pan underneath, and cook for 70 to 80 minutes. Begin basting with the reserved half of the marinade once the chicken reaches an internal temperature of 120°F (49°C), or the last half of the cooking time. Stop basting 10 minutes before taking the chicken off the grill. Once the chicken reaches an internal temperature of 175°F (80°C) in the thigh meat and 165°F (74°C) in the breast meat, remove from the grill.

6. Remove from the heat, carefully remove the rotisserie forks and slide the rod out, and then set the chicken on a large cutting board. Tent the chicken with aluminum foil and let it rest for 15 to 20 minutes before cutting off the twine and carving.

Barbecued Pulled Chicken

1 whole chicken,
3 to 3½ pounds (1.4 to 1.6 kg)

Basic Brine (page 50, optional)

1 medium onion, peeled but
left whole (for cavity)

Rub

2 teaspoons salt
(omit if brining the chicken)

2 teaspoons onion powder

2 teaspoons dried parsley

1 teaspoon paprika

1 teaspoon mustard powder

1 teaspoon mild chili powder

½ teaspoon garlic powder

¼ teaspoon celery salt

¼ teaspoon freshly
ground black pepper

Barbecue Sauce

¾ cup (180 ml) apple
cider vinegar

½ cup (120 g) ketchup

3 tablespoons (45 g)
packed brown sugar

2 teaspoons
Worcestershire sauce

½ teaspoon salt

⅛ teaspoon cayenne

1 tablespoon (14 g)
unsalted butter

Yield: 4 to 6 servings

Yes, pulled chicken can be made on the rotisserie. The self-basting action of the rotisserie helps keep the meat moist and easy to shred. We recommend brining the bird and cooking it a bit longer to help with the process. This chicken is perfect on sandwich buns with a side of coleslaw.

1. If brining the chicken, place it in a large resealable plastic bag or a plastic or glass container and place in the refrigerator for 4 hours. Make sure the chicken is completely submerged in the brine. Remove the chicken from the brine. Give it a quick rinse (do not over rinse) and pat dry inside and out with paper towels.

2. Prepare the grill for medium-high heat with indirect cooking.

3. Truss the chicken with kitchen twine. Run the rotisserie rod through the onion and insert it into the chicken cavity. Use a paring knife to cut a pilot hole in the onion to make this easier. Continue to run the rod through the chicken and secure with the rotisserie forks.

4. To make the rub: Combine the rub ingredients, omitting the salt if you brined the chicken, and apply evenly all over the chicken, making sure to get the seasoning under the breast skin and inside the body cavity.

5. Place the chicken on the preheated grill and set a drip pan underneath. Cook for 1½ hours, or until the meat in the thighs and legs reaches 175°F (80°C). The breasts should be 165°F (74°C).

6. To make the barbecue sauce: While the chicken is cooking, combine the barbecue sauce ingredients, except the butter, in a small saucepan over medium heat and simmer until the brown sugar has melted, about 5 minutes. Remove from the heat and stir in the butter. Let the sauce cool for 5 to 10 minutes.

7. Remove from the heat, carefully remove the rotisserie forks and slide the rod out, and then set the chicken on a large cutting board. Tent the chicken with aluminum foil and let it rest for 15 to 20 minutes before cutting off the twine and carving into manageable pieces. Shred the chicken, either by hand or with forks. Remove the skin, bones, and any bits of fat.

8. Transfer the sauce to a large pot and reheat on the stove for 1 to 2 minutes. Add the chicken, stir thoroughly, remove from the heat, and serve.

SMOKED ROTISSERIE TURKEY

1 whole turkey, 10 to
12 pounds (4.5 to 5.4 kg)

2 gallons (7.2 ml)
Basic Brine (page 50)

This recipe is best done on a charcoal grill, but a gas grill will work, too. However, it will not produce the same smoky flavor. In fact, it will pick up only a little smokiness. That is not to say that if this turkey is cooked on a gas grill it will not be delicious. We just feel you should understand the facts before you spend the 6 to 8 hours working on this recipe. That said, this is one of the best turkeys you will ever eat, with or without the smoke. The slow-roasting process guarantees a moist and tender bird. One last thing: Make sure that your rotisserie rod and motor can handle the size of the turkey you will be cooking.

1. Brine the turkey for 12 to 24 hours in the refrigerator or an ice-packed cooler. This will require a large container. Remove the turkey from the brine and rinse inside and out with cold water to remove excess salt. Do not over rinse. Pat dry inside and out with paper towels.

2. To make the rub: Combine the rub ingredients in a bowl and rub all over the turkey, getting under the breast skin and inside the cavity. Cover with plastic wrap and let sit for 15 to 20 minutes while you prepare the grill.

3. Prepare the grill for low heat with indirect cooking. The grill temperature should be held between 250°F and 300°F (121°C and 149°C) for the entire cooking time. Prepare to produce smoke during the cooking process (see page 22).

Rub

½ cup (56 g) paprika

2 tablespoons (14 g) freshly
ground black pepper

2 tablespoons (20 g) sugar

1 tablespoon (7 g)
onion powder

1 tablespoon (7 g)
mustard powder

2 teaspoons dried marjoram

1 teaspoon celery salt

½ teaspoon dried thyme

½ cup (112 g) unsalted
butter, melted

Yield: 8 servings

4. Truss the turkey with kitchen twine. Run the rotisserie rod through the turkey and tightly secure with the rotisserie forks. Balance as necessary. It may be necessary to tighten the placement of the turkey during the cooking time. Monitor to ensure that the turkey continues to turn and is cooking evenly.

5. Place the turkey on the preheated grill and set a drip pan underneath. Cook the turkey for approximately 6 hours, or until the internal temperature reaches 175°F to 185°F (80°C to 85°C) in the dark meat. It should be around 165°F to 175°F (74°C to 80°C) in the breast. Baste with the melted butter during the last 30 to 40 minutes of cooking time. Watch for burning.

6. Remove from the heat, carefully remove the rotisserie forks and slide the rod out, and then set the turkey on a large cutting board. Tent the turkey with aluminum foil and let it rest for 15 to 20 minutes before cutting off the twine and carving.

HONEY-MUSTARD TURKEY

1 whole turkey, 12 to 13 pounds (5.4 to 5.9 kg)

2 gallons (7.2 L) Basic Brine (page 50)

Glaze

½ cup (160 g) honey

¼ cup (45 g) Dijon mustard

1 tablespoon (15 ml) apple cider vinegar

½ teaspoon onion powder

½ teaspoon dried marjoram

¼ teaspoon ground nutmeg

Rub

2½ tablespoons (38 ml) olive oil

2 tablespoons (16 g) grated fresh ginger

2 tablespoons (12 g) freshly ground black pepper

3 or 4 cloves garlic, grated or minced

1 large onion, peeled but left whole (for cavity)

Yield: 10 servings

This turkey is suitable for any time of the year. If you're interested in a deliciously sweet, mustard-glazed turkey breast for sandwiches and casseroles, this is certainly your best bet. However, this dish is also perfect for holidays.

1. Brine the turkey for 12 to 24 hours in the refrigerator or an ice-packed cooler. This will require a large container.

2. To make the glaze: Warm the honey in a heatproof container in the microwave for 15 to 20 seconds. This will help liquefy it a bit. Stir well. Add the remaining glaze ingredients and mix thoroughly. Set aside.

3. Prepare the grill for medium heat with indirect cooking. Aim for a grill temperature of 325°F to 350°F (163°C to 177°C) the entire time. The cooking time for this turkey is 4 to 5 hours, so plan accordingly.

4. Remove the turkey from the brine and rinse inside and out with cold water. Pat dry inside and out with paper towels.

5. To make the rub: Combine all the ingredients in a small bowl and stir to form a paste. Rub all over the turkey, making sure to get some of the mixture under the breast skin. Truss the turkey with kitchen twine. Run the rotisserie rod through the onion and insert it into the turkey cavity. Use a paring knife to cut a pilot hole in the onion to make this easier. Continue to run the rod through the turkey and secure with the rotisserie forks.

6. Place the turkey on the grill and set a drip pan filled with water underneath. Grill for about 20 minutes per pound (454 g) or around 4 hours. Begin applying the glaze to the turkey after the second hour of the cooking time. The turkey is done when the thigh meat reaches 185°F (85°C) and the breast meat reaches 175°F (80°C).

7. Remove from the heat, carefully remove the rotisserie forks and slide the rod out, and then set the turkey on a large cutting board. Tent the turkey with aluminum foil and let it rest for 15 to 20 minutes before cutting off the twine and carving.

Pomegranate-Cranberry Glazed Turkey Breast

1 boneless turkey breast,
skin on, 3 to 3½ pounds
(1.4 to 1.6 kg)

1 gallon (3.7 L)
Basic Brine (page 50)

Rub

2 teaspoons mild chili powder

2 teaspoons freshly ground
black pepper

½ teaspoon dried oregano

½ teaspoon dried marjoram

¼ teaspoon ground allspice

⅛ teaspoon ground nutmeg

Baste

1¼ cups (295 ml) pure
cranberry juice

½ cup (120 g) pomegranate
preserves

½ cup (112 g) packed
dark brown sugar

2 tablespoons (30 ml)
white wine

1 tablespoon (15 ml) soy sauce

1 teaspoon Asian chili paste
(sambal sauce)

½ teaspoon grated fresh ginger

2 medium sprigs fresh thyme

2 tablespoons (28 g)
unsalted butter

Yield: 6 servings

One of the most unfortunate things about turkey is that most people only cook it once a year. This is our year-round favorite and it helps us keep our turkey grilling skills at their peak without having a refrigerator full of leftovers. By using a single turkey breast (you can tie two together it you like), we get just the right amount for dinner and a couple of leftover sandwiches the next day.

1. Brine the turkey breast for 3 hours in a large nonreactive container in the refrigerator.

2. To make the rub: Combine all the rub ingredients in a small bowl and set aside.

3. To make the baste: Place all the baste ingredients, except the butter, in a medium-size saucepan. Bring to a quick boil, decrease the heat to low, and simmer for 8 to 10 minutes. Make sure to keep an eye out for burning. Once the sauce coats the back of a spoon, remove from the heat and stir in the butter. Let cool to room temperature.

4. Prepare the grill for medium-high heat with indirect cooking.

5. Remove the turkey from the brine, rinse off the excess salt, and pat dry with paper towels. Apply the rub evenly all over the turkey. Run a long sword skewer through the center of the turkey lengthwise to create a pilot hole. Run the rotisserie rod through the hole and secure with the forks. Balance as necessary.

6. Place the turkey on the preheated grill, set a drip pan underneath, and add 2 cups (470 ml) hot water to the pan. Cook for 1½ hours, or until it reaches an internal temperature of 165°F (74°C). Baste with the pomegranate-cranberry mixture during the last 30 minutes of cooking time.

7. Remove from the heat, carefully remove the rotisserie forks and slide the rod out, and then set the turkey on a large cutting board. Tent the turkey with aluminum foil and let it rest for 15 to 20 minutes before carving into ¼- to ⅓-inch (6 to 8 mm) slices and serving.

Butter-Herb Turkey

1 whole turkey,
about 12 pounds (5.4 kg)

Basic Brine (page 50)

1 large onion, peeled but
left whole (for cavity)

⅓ cup (80 ml) olive oil

1 teaspoon freshly
ground black pepper

Baste

1 cup (2 sticks, 225 g)
unsalted butter

3 cloves garlic, minced

1 small shallot, finely chopped

¼ cup (15 g) chopped
flat-leaf parsley

1 tablespoon (2.5 g)
chopped fresh sage

1 tablespoon (2.5 g)
chopped fresh basil

1 ½ teaspoons chopped
fresh thyme

Yield: 8 servings

This is a fantastic holiday turkey. As with our other poultry recipes, this will need to brined. Make sure you have the needed time, materials, and space for this task. This buttery turkey will be juicy, tender, and impressive. The leftovers are perfect for sandwiches and soup.

1. Brine the turkey for 18 to 24 hours in the refrigerator or an ice-packed cooler. This will require a large container.

2. Prepare the grill for medium heat with indirect cooking. Aim for a grill temperature of 325°F to 350°F (163°C to 177°C) the entire time. The cooking time for this turkey is 4 to 5 hours, so plan accordingly.

3. Remove the turkey from the brine and rinse with cold water. Do not over rinse. Pat dry inside and out with paper towels. Truss the turkey with kitchen twine. Run the rotisserie rod through the onion and insert it into the turkey cavity. Use a paring knife to cut a pilot hole in the onion to make this easier. Continue to run the rod through the turkey and secure with the rotisserie forks. Brush the turkey well with the olive oil and season with the pepper. Place the turkey on the grill, set a drip pan underneath, and add 2 cups (470 ml) hot water to the pan.

4. To make the baste: While the turkey is cooking, melt the butter in a saucepan over medium heat and add the garlic and shallot. Lightly simmer for 2 minutes. Remove from the heat and add all the herbs. Let the mixture sit for 5 minutes.

5. Begin basting the turkey after the first hour of cooking time. Do so every 30 minutes until the turkey is almost done. The cooking time for this turkey should be 20 minutes per pound (454 g), or about 4 hours. The turkey is done when the thigh meat reaches 185°F (85°C) and the breast meat reaches 175°F (80°C).

6. Remove from the heat, carefully remove the rotisserie forks and slide the rod out, and then set the turkey on a large cutting board. Tent the turkey with aluminum foil and let it rest for 20 minutes before cutting off the twine and carving. This will give you time to make gravy or finish any drip pan recipes. Slice and serve.

BACON-WRAPPED TURKEY BREAST

1 whole skinless, boneless turkey breast, 2½ to 3 pounds (1.1 to 1.4 kg)

Basic Brine (page 50)

Glaze

¼ cup (65 g) apricot preserves

2 teaspoons chopped fresh rosemary

½ teaspoon freshly ground black pepper

6 to 8 strips bacon

Yield: 4 to 6 servings

This is a simple bacon-wrapped turkey breast recipe basted with a rosemary-apricot glaze. Really, this dish is perfect for any time of the year but fancy enough for the holidays. We've found that the leftovers make delicious sandwiches, too.

1. Brine the turkey breast for 4 to 5 hours in a large nonreactive container.

2. Prepare the grill for medium-high heat with indirect cooking.

3. To make the glaze: Place the glaze ingredients in a small saucepan over medium heat and heat through for 2 minutes. Remove and let cool for 10 to 15 minutes.

4. Remove the turkey from the brine, rinse with cold water, and pat dry with paper towels. Brush half of the glaze mixture onto the turkey breast and wrap with the bacon slices (which the glaze should help hold in place. Using kitchen twine, tie the bacon to the turkey at 1-inch (2.5 cm) intervals while working to form the turkey breast into a consistent round shape. Run a long sword skewer through the center of the turkey lengthwise to create a pilot hole. Run the rotisserie rod through the hole and secure with the forks. Balance as necessary.

5. Place the turkey on the preheated grill, set a drip pan underneath, and add 2 cups (470 ml) hot water to the pan. Cook for 80 to 90 minutes, or until the thickest part of the breast reaches 175°F (80°C). Baste with the remaining glaze after the first 40 minutes of cooking. You will only need to apply the glaze one or twice. Do not glaze past 60 minutes.

6. Remove from the heat, carefully remove the rotisserie forks and slide the rod out, and then set the turkey on a large cutting board. Tent the turkey with aluminum foil and let it rest for 10 to 12 minutes before cutting off the twine and carving into ½-inch (1.3 cm)-thick slices. Serve with your favorite side dishes.

Wild Rice–Stuffed Turkey Breast

This vintage stuffed turkey recipe is absolutely perfect for any time of the year, especially for Sunday dinner and small holiday gatherings. What makes it even more festive is the deeply nostalgic flavor of the sticky orange glaze.

1 skinless, boneless turkey breast, about 3 pounds (1.4 kg)

Basic Brine (page 50)

Filling

1 cup (160 g) wild rice mix

1½ cups (355 ml) chicken broth

1 tablespoon (15 ml) olive oil

1 large leek, washed well and finely chopped

2 cloves garlic, minced

1 tablespoon (4 g) chopped fresh oregano

½ teaspoon chopped fresh thyme

¼ teaspoon salt

¼ teaspoon freshly ground black pepper

¼ cup (30 g) dried cranberries

Glaze

1 cup (235 g) orange marmalade

Zest and juice of 1 orange

2 tablespoons (30 ml) balsamic vinegar

2 teaspoons soy sauce

Pinch of salt (optional)

Yield: 4 to 6 servings

1. Brine the turkey breast in a nonreactive container for 3 to 4 hours in the refrigerator.

2. To make the filling: Cook the wild rice mix in the chicken broth as directed on the package. Heat the oil in a large skillet over medium heat and cook the leek for 5 to 6 minutes, until it has wilted down a bit and begins to look translucent. Add the garlic and cook for 30 seconds. Transfer the cooked rice to the skillet with the oregano, thyme, salt, and pepper. Cook for about 3 minutes. Remove from the heat, add the dried cranberries, stir to combine, and let the rice cool for 15 minutes.

3. While rice is cooling prepare the glaze: Combine the glaze ingredients in a saucepan and simmer over medium heat for 3 minutes, or until the marmalade has melted. Remove from the heat and let cool.

4. Prepare the grill for medium-high heat with indirect cooking.

5. Remove the turkey from the brine, rinse with cold water, and pat dry with paper towels. Lay the turkey breast on a large cutting board. Cut halfway through the breast and roll it open. Make a series of cuts into the meat, but not all the way through. Spread the stuffing over the cut surface of the turkey. Roll together into a uniform shape and tie with kitchen twine. Start by tying on the ends and work toward the center. Replace any stuffing that falls out. Carefully thread onto the rotisserie rod and secure with the forks.

6. Place the stuffed turkey breast on the preheated grill, set a drip pan underneath, and add 2 cups (470 ml) hot water to the pan. Cook for 1 to 1½ hours, or until the thickest part of the breast reaches 175°F (80°C). Apply the glaze during the last half of the cooking time. Do this about 4 or 5 times, or every 10 minutes, until the turkey is done.

7. Remove from the heat, carefully remove the rotisserie forks and slide the rod out, and then set the turkey breast on a large cutting board. Tent the turkey with aluminum foil and let it rest for 7 minutes before cutting off the twine and carving into ½-inch (1.3 cm)-thick pieces. Some of the filling might escape during the cutting process. Don't despair: just repack the spaces as needed.

QUICK AND EASY GAME HENS

Marinade

¼ cup (60 ml) olive oil

Juice of 3 lemons

Zest of 1 lemon

3 cloves garlic, minced

1½ teaspoons salt,
plus more as needed

½ teaspoon freshly
ground black pepper,
plus more as needed

¼ teaspoon dried thyme

4 game hens,
1 to 1½ pounds
(454 to 680 g) each

Salt and pepper

Yield: 4 servings

The name says it all. These game hens require only a short marinating time and then it's onto the rotisserie for a quick cook. Small birds like this don't take very long to cook, so you can have dinner on the table in a short time.

1. To make the marinade: Combine the marinade ingredients in a measuring cup. Place 2 birds into one resealable plastic bag and pour half of the mixture over the top. Repeat the process with the second set of birds and the remaining marinade. Seal the bags and place in the refrigerator for 30 to 45 minutes.

2. Prepare the grill for medium-high heat with indirect cooking.

3. Remove the birds from the marinade and season with a little more salt and pepper. Truss the birds with kitchen twine. Run the rotisserie rod through all 4 birds, push them together, and secure with the forks. Game hens will lock together if each one is turned 90 degrees relative to the others.

4. Place the birds on the grill, set a drip pan underneath, and add 2 cups (470 ml) hot water to the pan. Cook for 40 to 45 minutes, or until the internal temperature of the thigh meat reaches 185°F (85°C) and at least 165°F (74°C) in the breast.

5. Remove from the heat, carefully remove the rotisserie forks and slide the rod out, and then set the hens on a large cutting board. Tent the birds with aluminum foil and let rest for 10 minutes. Cut off the twine. Serve whole or cut in half vertically through the backbone and serve in halves.

SHERRY AND SOY GAME HENS

Marinade

⅔ cup (160 ml) dry sherry

⅓ cup (80 ml) soy sauce

2 or 3 cloves garlic, minced

1 tablespoon (12 g) sugar

2 teaspoons finely chopped fresh ginger

¼ teaspoon salt

¼ teaspoon white pepper

4 game hens, 1 to 1½ pounds (454 to 680 g) each

Yield: 4 servings

Game hens seem a novelty item these days, but they really are a great way to enjoy a fantastic chicken in a new package. The first recommendation we make with game hens is to look for a little better quality than most stores tend to carry. Ask around and check out some specialty markets for good-quality Cornish game hens. Then try this recipe, which yields an incredibly tender and flavorful bird.

1. To make the marinade: Combine the marinade ingredients in a measuring cup. Place 2 birds into one resealable plastic bag and pour half of the mixture over the top. Repeat the process with the second set of birds and the remaining marinade. Seal the bags and place in the refrigerator for 3 to 4 hours.

2. Prepare the grill for medium-high heat with indirect cooking.

3. Remove the birds from the marinade and tie the legs together with kitchen twine. Run the rotisserie rod through all 4 birds, push them together, and secure with the forks. Game hens will lock together if each one is turned 90 degrees relative to the others.

4. Place the birds on the grill, set a drip pan underneath, and add 2 cups (470 ml) hot water to the pan. Cook for 40 to 45 minutes, or until the internal temperature of the thigh meat reaches 185°F (85°C) and at least 165°F (74°C) in the breast.

5. Remove from the heat, carefully remove the rotisserie forks and slide the rod out, and then set the hens on a large cutting board. Tent the birds with aluminum foil and let rest for 10 minutes. Cut off the twine. Serve whole or cut in half vertically through the backbone and serve in halves.

CHAPTER 6

ROTISSERIE BASKET COOKING

The rotisserie is built for slow cooking large foods like roasts and whole poultry, but it can also be used for preparing smaller items with the addition of a rotisserie basket. We particularly like tumble basket chicken wings because they turn out crispy on the outside and tender on the inside. Plus, they can be cooked in as little as 30 minutes, though we like a lower and slower cooking time to get the most of the open-flame flavor.

Rotisserie baskets come in two types, the tumble basket and the flat basket. Flat baskets are the perfect choice for those in-between items, such as chicken legs and thighs, smaller cuts of meat like steaks (a recipe you simply must try), and many types of vegetables. Flat baskets work by compressing the food into a base with a flat grate section. Generally, they can accommodate any item from ½ to 2 inches (1.3 to 5 cm) in thickness. These baskets tend to be about 14 inches (35.6) long and 7 inches (17.8 cm) wide and fit most full-size grills, including most charcoal units that have rotisserie attachments.

1. Trim the salmon steaks.

2. Fold in the ends.

3. Wrap around the perimeter.

4. Tie and cut the excess twine.

5. Place the tied steaks into a flat basket.

Tumble baskets are cylindrical-shaped units that attach to the rotisserie rod. Food tumbles around inside of them as the rotisserie turns. These are perfect for smaller items, but not too small. Although there are some much more expensive tumble baskets that can turn even coffee beans (for doing your own roasting), most of them have wide gaps that allow smaller food items to fall through. Large Brussels sprouts, small potatoes, and whole chicken wings work perfectly in these baskets and the constant rotation ensures even cooking. When choosing items to put in a tumble basket, test them against the gaps in the wires to make sure they are not going to fall through. An hour of turning will give these items every possible chance to do so.

Basket cooking is similar to any other form of grilling. While most of the items placed into one of these two basket types can be grilled directly on the cooking grates, the same rotisserie advantages work here just as well. Basket-grilled foods will cook evenly with little intervention from the cook. These are great solutions for poultry in particular, where flare-ups can be an issue. When using a rotisserie basket, grill indirectly and, provided there is sufficient space, place a drip pan underneath.

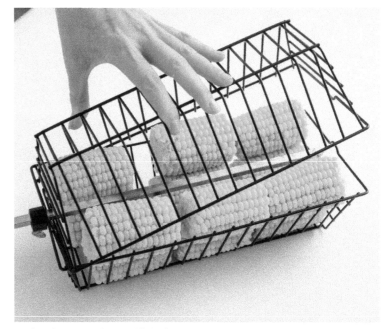

1. Place the corn inside a tumble basket and insert the rotisserie rod.

2. Secure the tumble basket.

Smoked Rib-Eye Steaks

Rub

1 tablespoon (15 ml) olive oil

1 tablespoon (18 g) kosher salt

2 cloves garlic, minced

2 teaspoons apple cider vinegar

1 teaspoon onion powder

½ teaspoon smoked paprika

½ teaspoon freshly ground black pepper

½ teaspoon ground cumin

½ teaspoon dried oregano

½ teaspoon mild chili powder

2 large, thick-cut, boneless rib-eye steaks, 1 to 1¼ inches (2.5 to 3.1 cm) thick

Yield: 2 servings

Smoked steaks are the most flavorful and tender steaks you'll ever try. They are simple to prepare and this has quickly become one of our favorite steak recipes. We recommend doing this over charcoal, but if you have a gas unit, don't despair, as you can always build a smoke packet (see page 22). These steaks go against everything you have ever heard about grilling. They are cooked low and slow to a high internal temperature, but they are smoky in flavor and amazingly tender.

1. To make the rub: Combine the rub ingredients in a small bowl and apply to both sides of the steak. Cover with plastic wrap and place in the refrigerator for 4 to 6 hours.

2. Remove the steaks from the refrigerator and let sit at room temperature for 20 to 30 minutes.

3. Prepare the grill for medium heat with indirect cooking. Prepare to produce smoke during the cooking process (see page 22).

4. Place the steaks in a flat basket and secure onto the rotisserie rod. Place on the preheated grill. Cook for 30 to 40 minutes, or until the steaks reach an internal temperature of 160°F (71°C).

5. Remove from the heat and carefully take the steaks out of the basket. Place the steaks on a cutting board and loosely tent with aluminum foil. Let the meat rest for 15 minutes. Either slice the steaks or serve whole.

Pomegranate-Teriyaki Beef Short Ribs

Marinade

1 cup (235 ml) tamari soy sauce or dark soy sauce

½ cup (112 g) packed brown sugar

¼ cup (80 g) pomegranate molasses

2 or 3 scallions, finely chopped (both white and green parts)

4 cloves garlic, minced

1 tablespoon (15 ml) oyster sauce

2 teaspoons Worcestershire sauce

2 teaspoons mirin

1 teaspoon vegetable oil

1 teaspoon grated fresh ginger

1 teaspoon Asian chili sauce

6 beef short ribs, 3½ to 4 inches (8.9 to 10 cm) long and 2 inches (5 cm) thick

Chopped scallion, for garnish

⅓ cup (65 g) pomegranate seeds, for garnish

Yield: 4 to 6 servings

Short ribs are without a doubt a deeply rich and flavorful cut of beef. They do tend to be a little fatty, though, so we recommend cooking these low and slow to render some of that fat. Serve these delicious, tender morsels over rice or steamed vegetables. We've found that the leftovers are easily shredded and added to sandwiches, soups, or stews, or served over noodles.

1. To make the marinade: Combine the marinade ingredients in a saucepan and simmer over medium heat for 3 to 5 minutes, until the sugar has dissolved, stirring occasionally. Remove from the heat and let the mixture cool for 30 minutes. Divide the marinade into two equal portions. Store one half in the refrigerator for basting. Use the remaining half as the marinade.

2. Trim off any excess fat or straggling meat from the surface of the ribs. Do not attempt to remove any internal fat. Place the ribs in a resealable plastic bag and add the marinade. Using tongs, gently turn the ribs to coat. Seal the bag and place in the refrigerator for 6 to 12 hours.

3. Prepare the grill for medium heat with indirect cooking.

4. Set a tumble basket on a large cutting board. This will keep your floors and countertop clean. Remove the ribs from the bag and place them in the basket. Discard any marinade left in the bag. Secure the basket.

5. Place the basket on the preheated grill with a drip pan underneath, making sure that it doesn't get in the way of the basket as it turns. Cook for 1 to 1½ hours, or until the ribs have rendered the majority of their fat and have reached an internal temperature of 170°F to 180°F (77°C to 82°C).

6. Heat the reserved marinade in a bowl in the microwave for 1 minute. Stir. Begin basting with this mixture during the last 20 to 30 minutes of cooking time.

7. Remove the basket from the grill and place on a heat-resistant cutting board. Let the ribs rest for 5 minutes or so. Carefully open the basket and plate the ribs. Serve garnished with the chopped scallion and pomegranate seeds.

Rotisserie Basket Sausage, Peppers, and Onions

6 to 8 bratwurst sausages

2 large bell peppers, halved and seeded

1 large onion, halved through the stem end, stem left intact

6 to 8 sub rolls

Grainy mustard, for serving

Yield: 6 to 8 servings

This is a quick and simple way to prepare the fixings for a sausage sandwich on the grill. Since all of the ingredients are placed together in the flat basket, there is no need to worry about separate cooking times. All of the items are cooked through at the same rate, which streamlines the process.

1. Prepare the grill for medium-high heat with indirect cooking.

2. Put the sausages, peppers, and onions in a flat basket and secure onto the rotisserie rod. Place on the preheated grill and cook for 20 to 25 minutes. These cook fairly quickly, so we recommend checking the internal temperature of the sausages after they've been on for 15 minutes; they are ready when the internal temperature reaches 165°F (74°C).

3. Remove the basket from the grill and remove the contents from the basket. Transfer the cooked onions and peppers to a cutting board and slice them into strips. Warm the sub rolls. Place the sausages, onions, and peppers into the warmed sub rolls and top with a good-quality grainy mustard.

Sriracha Chicken Leg Quarters

Marinade

¼ cup (60 ml) Sriracha

¼ cup (80 g) honey

2 tablespoons (30 ml) oyster sauce

2 tablespoons (30 ml) soy sauce

2 cloves garlic, minced

1 teaspoon grated fresh ginger

¼ teaspoon salt

¼ teaspoon white pepper

4 chicken leg quarters, skin on

Toasted sesame seeds or finely chopped scallion, for garnish

Yield: 4 servings

Without a doubt, you'll make this rotisserie chicken again and again. These leg quarters are sweet, spicy, juicy, and absolutely drool worthy. If you cannot get your hands on leg quarters, use either thighs or drumsticks and double the amount.

1. To make the marinade: In a bowl, stir together the marinade ingredients until everything is well incorporated. Divide the mixture in half, reserving half to use as a baste.

2. Cut off any straggling skin from the leg quarters and score two ¼-inch (6 mm)-deep cuts across the leg and thigh portions. Place the chicken into a resealable plastic bag and add the marinade. Seal the bag and gently toss to coat. Place in the refrigerator for 30 minutes to 1 hour.

3. Prepare the grill for medium-high heat with indirect cooking.

4. Remove the marinated chicken from the bag, discard the marinade, place the chicken in a flat basket, and secure the chicken onto the rotisserie rod. Cook for 45 to 60 minutes, or until the internal temperature at the thickest part of the meat reaches 175°F (80°C). During the last 25 minutes of cooking time, begin basting with the reserved marinade. Do this about 4 times until the chicken is fully cooked.

5. Remove the basket from the grill and carefully remove the chicken from the basket. Set it onto a serving dish or cutting board. Let the meat rest for about 5 minutes. Sprinkle with the sesame seeds or chopped scallion and serve.

CHURRASCO CHICKEN LEGS

Marinade

⅓ cup (80 ml) white wine vinegar or freshly squeezed lime juice

2 tablespoons (30 ml) water

1 tablespoon (15 ml) olive oil

4 cloves garlic, minced

2 teaspoons paprika (not smoked)

1¼ teaspoons salt

½ teaspoon dried thyme

¼ teaspoon cayenne pepper, or to taste

¼ teaspoon freshly ground black pepper

4 chicken leg quarters, skin on

¼ cup (16 g) roughly chopped flat-leaf parsley, for garnish

Yield: 4 servings

This is a loose take on the churrasco chicken served in Brazilian restaurants. We found it easier to use a flat basket for this recipe, as it holds the chicken leg quarters in place. Serve this dish together with the Churrasco Beef (page 83) for larger cookouts.

1. To make the marinade: Combine the marinade ingredients in a small bowl.

2. Score two ¼-inch (6 mm)-deep cuts across the leg and thigh portions. Place in a resealable plastic bag and pour the marinade over the top. Release air from the bag, seal, and, in light squeezing motions, work the marinade all over the chicken pieces. Place in the refrigerator for 4 to 6 hours.

3. Preheat the grill for medium-high heat with indirect cooking.

4. Remove the chicken from the bag, discard the marinade, place it in a flat basket, and secure the basket onto the rotisserie rod. Set a drip pan underneath if there is space. If not, use a piece of aluminum foil instead.

5. Cook the leg quarters for 60 to 75 minutes, or until the thickest part of the thigh reaches an internal temperature of 175°F (80°C).

6. Remove the basket from the grill. Remove the chicken from the basket and place it on a serving platter. Tent with aluminum foil and let the chicken rest for 10 minutes. Serve garnished with the parsley.

Barbecued Chicken Leg Quarters

4 large chicken leg quarters, skin on

Basic Brine (page 50)

Barbecue Sauce

1 cup (240 g) ketchup

½ cup (120 g) apple jelly (not apple butter)

2 tablespoons (30 ml) apple cider vinegar

½ teaspoon onion powder

¼ teaspoon mild chili powder

¼ teaspoon salt

½ teaspoon freshly ground black pepper

⅛ teaspoon ground allspice

Rub

2 teaspoons dried marjoram

1 teaspoon onion powder

1 teaspoon mustard powder

1 teaspoon freshly ground black pepper

1 teaspoon mild chili powder

½ teaspoon garlic powder

Yield: 4 servings

The problem with grilling chicken is the flare-ups. The fat below the skin on chicken legs and thighs melts away quickly into a highly combustible liquid. And let's be honest—these pieces benefit more from a slower roast than a hot and fast direct grill. Our answer to barbecued chicken is a rotisserie basket and a great rub, followed by an even better sauce. This recipe works best with a flat-style rotisserie basket.

1. Brine the chicken for 4 hours in a large resealable bag or a plastic or glass container in the refrigerator. Make sure the chicken is completely submerged in the brine.

2. To make the barbecue sauce: Combine the barbecue sauce ingredients in a saucepan over medium heat and simmer for 5 to 6 minutes. Stir occasionally and watch for burning. Decrease the heat if necessary. Let the sauce cool before using.

3. Remove the chicken from the brine. Give it a quick rinse and pat dry with paper towels. Trim any loose skin and excessive fat from the chicken. Cut one slit through the skin in the drumstick portion and two through the thigh section.

4. To make the rub: Combine the rub ingredients in a small bowl and apply all over the chicken leg quarters, getting it under the skin where possible. Cover loosely with plastic wrap and set aside while you prepare the grill.

5. Prepare the grill for medium-high heat with indirect cooking. Set a drip pan underneath if there is space, or use aluminum foil instead.

6. Place the chicken leg quarter into a flat rotisserie basket and secure tightly. It may be necessary to tighten during cooking so watch carefully. Secure the basket on the rotisserie rod. Cook for 30 to 45 minutes, testing for doneness in the thickest part of each leg. During the last 10 minutes of the cooking time, brush the barbecue sauce onto the chicken. This is a little awkward working through the rotisserie basket, but get the coating as evenly as possible. Dark meat should be cooked to 175°F (80°C).

7. Remove the basket from the grill and the chicken from the basket. Tent with aluminum foil and let rest for 5 minutes before serving.

Tandoori Chicken Legs

4 chicken leg quarters, skin on

Marinade

1 cup (240 g) plain yogurt
(do not use Greek yogurt)

Juice of 2 large limes

2½ teaspoons salt

2¼ teaspoons ground cumin

2¼ teaspoons onion powder

3 cloves garlic, minced

1¼ teaspoons
ground coriander

½ teaspoon freshly
ground black pepper

½ teaspoon Indian chili
powder or cayenne

½ teaspoon ground fenugreek

½ teaspoon ground cardamom

3 or 4 drops red food coloring

Chopped fresh cilantro,
for garnish

Sliced red onion, for garnish

Yield: 4 servings

This is one of the best ways to cook tandoori chicken. Although it is traditionally cooked in a tandoor, the rotisserie method keeps the meat tender and juicy, while the grill offers a similar open-flame flavor. This recipe works well on both charcoal and gas units and uses a flat rotisserie basket.

1. Remove the skins from the chicken leg quarters. With a knife, score two ⅛-inch (3 mm)-deep cuts across the leg and thigh portions. Place the legs into a large resealable plastic bag.

2. To make the marinade: Combine the marinade ingredients in a bowl, leaving the red food coloring for last. It will take on a pink hue. That is normal. Reserve one-third of the marinade, for basting, in an airtight container in the refrigerator until ready to use. Pour the remaining marinade over the chicken and, using kitchen tongs, gently turn the chicken to coat. Release air from the bag, seal, and place in the refrigerator for 6 to 12 hours.

3. Prepare the grill for medium-high heat with indirect cooking.

4. Remove the reserved marinade from the refrigerator and let sit at room temperature for at least 15 minutes to bring its temperature up.

5. Set a flat rotisserie basket on a large cutting board. Place the marinated chicken in the basket. Secure the basket onto the rotisserie rod and carefully take out to the grill with the cutting board still underneath.

6. Place the basket onto the preheated grill and make sure that it can turn freely. Brush on the reserved marinade during the first 20 minutes of cooking time. Repeat the process 2 or 3 times. Cook the chicken until it reaches an internal temperature of 185°F to 190°F (85°C to 88°C). This temperature closely reproduces both the texture and the flavor of traditional tandoori chicken.

7. Remove from the heat and set the basket on a clean, heat-resistant cutting board. Be careful because the basket will be very hot. Let the meat rest for 5 to 10 minutes. Carefully remove the chicken and serve topped with the chopped cilantro and sliced red onion.

Tumble Basket Hot Wings

2 pounds (910 g)
whole chicken wings

Marinade

¼ cup (60 ml) olive oil

⅔ cup (160 ml) white vinegar

1 or 2 red chiles,
finely chopped

1 tablespoon (18 g) kosher salt

Rub

1 teaspoon onion powder

1 teaspoon freshly
ground black pepper

½ teaspoon garlic powder

½ teaspoon cayenne,
or to taste

¼ teaspoon mild chili powder

Yield: 4 servings

If you haven't tried rotisserie-style hot wings, you are in for a treat. Not only are these nicely spiced, but the vinegar and rotating action of the rotisserie also help crisp up the chicken in about 30 minutes. No need to fry the wings. This recipe does not call for a sauce, so if you'd like to add one, do so at the very end. To be honest, they really don't need it.

1. Cut the tips off of the whole wings and discard. Place the wings in a resealable plastic bag.

2. To make the marinade: Combine the marinade ingredients in s small bowl. Pour the marinade over the top of the chicken, release air from the bag, seal, and, in light squeezing motions, work the marinade all over the meat. Place in the refrigerator for 4 hours.

3. Prepare the grill for medium-high heat with indirect cooking.

4. Remove the wings from the bag and place into a bowl or on a cutting board.

5. To make the rub: Combine the rub ingredients in a small bowl and apply to the wings. Place the wings in a tumble basket and secure the basket. It is best to set something underneath the basket, since this can get a little messy.

6. Secure the basket to the rotisserie rod and cook for 30 to 35 minutes. The wings should be nice and crispy and must reach an internal temperature of at least 175°F (80°C). It is okay to let the wings go to 185°F (85°C) for crispier wings.

7. Remove the basket from the grill. Remove the wings from the basket and set on a large cutting board. Carefully cut the wings in half, dividing the drummettes from the flats. Serve as is or with a sauce on the side.

Orange-Teriyaki Salmon Steaks

Marinade

¼ cup (60 ml) soy sauce

¼ cup (60 ml) freshly squeezed orange juice

3 tablespoons (45 g) packed brown sugar

2 scallions, white parts only, finely chopped

2 cloves garlic, minced

2 teaspoons sherry

1 teaspoon sesame oil

½ teaspoon grated fresh ginger

¼ teaspoon white pepper

Pinch of salt

2 salmon steaks, 1 to 1¼ inches (2.5 to 3.1 cm) thick

2 scallions, green parts only, chopped, for garnish

Yield: 2 to 4 servings

Salmon steaks are perfect for the grill given their shape and texture. This recipe calls for the salmon to be placed in a flat basket and cooked rotisserie style. The end result is a tender, juicy, amazing fish. With salmon steaks, watch out for the bones in the center. You can try to pull them out before cooking, but this can be difficult and can cause tearing. It is much easier to remove the bones after the fish has been cooked. So before you serve this fantastic fish, remove the bones.

1. To make the marinade: Combine the marinade ingredients in a small saucepan over medium heat and simmer for 3 to 4 minutes, stirring often. Remove from the heat and let cool for 30 minutes.

2. The way salmon steaks are shaped, there are two prongs of meat at the bottom. On the inner edge of that meat there is a thin film. Take a paring knife and carefully cut that away. Place the salmon steaks in a resealable plastic bag. Pour the cooled marinade over the fish, making sure all the surfaces are well coated. Seal the bag and place in the refrigerator for 2 hours.

3. Prepare the grill for medium-high heat with indirect cooking.

4. Remove the fish from the bag and discard the marinade. Fold one end of the prongs in and the other end around it, creating a circle. Tie the outside perimeter with kitchen twine. This process will help keep the salmon steaks intact as they cook, or they will break apart from the movement of the rotisserie unit. Place the salmon steaks in a flat basket and secure.

5. Secure the basket to the rotisserie rod. Cook the fish until it reaches an internal temperature of 145°F (63°C), 15 to 18 minutes.

6. Remove the basket from the grill and carefully remove the salmon from the basket. Let the fish rest for a few minutes. Carefully remove the center bone structure from the steaks. Cut off the twine. Serve whole or divide in half lengthwise for smaller portions. Garnish with the chopped scallions before serving.

Barbecue Spice–Rubbed Salmon Steaks

1 lemon

3 medium salmon steaks, each about 8 ounces (225 g) and 1½ inches (3.8 cm) thick

Rub

1 tablespoon (15 g) packed brown sugar

2 teaspoons mild chili powder

1½ teaspoons onion powder

1 teaspoon dried parsley

½ teaspoon salt

½ teaspoon freshly ground black pepper

¼ teaspoon smoked paprika

¼ teaspoon garlic powder

Yield: 3 to 6 servings

One of our favorite pieces of salmon is the steak. The meat is much more tender and flavorful and it holds together well in the flat basket. These salmon steaks are rubbed with a barbecue-inspired seasoning and cooked to perfection.

1. Prepare the grill for medium-high heat with indirect cooking.

2. Cut the lemon in half and squeeze the juice over both sides of the salmon steaks. Let sit for 3 minutes. Pat dry with paper towels. The way salmon steaks are shaped, there are two prongs of meat at the bottom. On the inner edge of that meat there is a thin film. Take a paring knife and carefully cut that away. Fold one end in and the other end around it, creating a circle. Tie the outside perimeter with kitchen twine. This process will help keep the salmon steaks intact as they cook, or they will break apart from the movement of the rotisserie unit.

3. To make the rub: Combine the rub ingredients in a small bowl and apply to the exposed fish on both sides. Place in a flat basket and secure. Secure the basket to the rotisserie rod.

4. Place on the preheated grill and cook for 18 to 20 minutes, or until the internal temperature of the fish reaches 145°F (63°C).

5. Carefully remove the basket from the rotisserie and remove the fish from the basket. Place on a cutting board. Carefully remove the large bone structure located in the center of the steaks. This should be fairly easy to do. Cut off the twine and serve the steaks. You may also cut the steaks in half vertically and serve in smaller portions.

RED SNAPPER WITH JERK SEASONINGS

1 small red chile, finely chopped

¼ cup (60 ml) olive oil

Juice of 2 limes

1 whole red snapper, about 2½ pounds (965 g)

Rub

1 teaspoon coarse salt

1 teaspoon chopped fresh thyme

2½ teaspoons olive oil

1 clove garlic, minced

½ teaspoon freshly ground black pepper

½ teaspoon sugar

¼ teaspoon ground allspice

¼ teaspoon ground cinnamon

¼ teaspoon ground nutmeg

¼ teaspoon cayenne, or to taste

1 lime, sliced

¼ onion, sliced

Lime juice, for serving (optional)

Yield: 2 to 4 servings

Red snapper is a must-try fish, but it can be hard to get your hands on in some locations. If you happen to find a whole snapper, then give this recipe a whirl. The fish takes on a Caribbean flair when seasoned with a Jamaican jerk spice rub. Serve with coconut rice and a delicious rum cocktail.

1. Prepare the grill for medium heat with indirect cooking.

2. Place the chopped chile in a bowl, pour over the olive oil, and let sit for 10 minutes. Sprinkle the lime juice on the outside and inside of the fish.

3. To make the rub: Combine the rub ingredients in a small bowl and apply to the interior of the fish. Layer the lime and onion slices on the inside and tie the fish with kitchen twine in two places. Brush the exterior of the fish with the chile oil. Put the fish into a flat basket and secure.

4. Secure the basket to the rotisserie rod and cook the fish for 20 minutes, or until the fish reaches an internal temperature of 145°F (63°C).

5. Remove the basket from the grill and remove the fish from the basket. Transfer the fish to a cutting board and let sit for 5 minutes.

6. Cut off the twine. Discard the lime slices but keep the onions. If desired, sprinkle with freshly squeezed lime juice just before serving. This fish can also be flaked and added to dips or fish fritters.

ROTISSERIE BASKET TROUT

3 whole trout, 10 to 12 ounces
(280 to 336 g) each, cleaned

¾ teaspoon salt

½ teaspoon freshly
ground black pepper

9 sprigs fresh oregano

3 sprigs fresh thyme

9 lemon slices

3 lemon wedges

Yield: 6 servings

There are few things better than fresh-caught trout cooking over a campfire. For those who don't have the opportunity to spend a day by the stream, this is the next best thing. The grill simulates that fire perfectly and a rotisserie basket keeps the fish out of the fire and allows them to roast to perfection. Add a little smoke if you like (see page 22), but either way, these trout are delicious.

1. Prepare the grill for medium-high to high heat with indirect cooking.

2. Season the inside of each trout with salt and pepper. In the cavity of each fish, place 3 sprigs of oregano, 1 sprig of thyme, and 3 slices of lemon.

3. Tie each trout with kitchen twine, place in a rotisserie basket, and secure. Attach to the rotisserie rod, making sure the basket is closed tightly and the trout do not move around.

4. Place the fish on the preheated grill and cook for 20 to 30 minutes, or until the internal temperature of the fish reaches 145°F (63°C). Watch for burning and decrease the heat if necessary.

5. Remove the basket from the grill and carefully remove the fish from the basket. Let cool for 5 to 10 minutes. Carefully separate the skin from the fillet and lift away the bones. The bones should pull away easily, but some bones will be left behind, so examine carefully. The fish should flake easily. Serve each fillet with a lemon wedge.

CHAPTER 7

SIDE DISHES

Most of the time, the rotisserie is going to be busy cooking the main dish, but that doesn't mean that it can't be used for a side dish, or a side dish can't be prepared simultaneously with that main course. All the advantages that make a large roast or a whole poultry perfect on the rotisserie will work with large vegetables or fruit, like a head of cabbage or a pineapple. The roasting capabilities can turn items like these into the perfect side dish or even dessert. Use the same rules and start with a rub or marinade before the food goes on the grill and it will have all the flavors you are looking for. Since vegetables cook quickly, these side dishes can be done while many large meat items are resting before carving.

Another great way to prepare a side dish with rotisserie items is in the drip pan. Drip pans help keep the grill clean, but can also be used for cooking. Even though the burners beneath the pan are not being used, the grill is still hot enough to slow roast a wide range of items, basted and seasoned by whatever is turning on the rotisserie above. Hearty vegetables, such as potatoes and fall squash, are perfect for the drip pan, but most anything can be cooked here. This allows for a complete meal to be made with only the grill, keeping the cooking outside. Even better, you can divide a pan in half with a sheet of foil and make two drip pan dishes at the same time.

Since many drip pan items will cook faster than the large cut of meat above, it may be necessary to either add the drip pan items later or switch out the drip pan while cooking. Be safe and use fire-resistant gloves to make this operation quick and easy. If the roast or poultry on the rotisserie is relatively lean and the drippings are not excessively fatty, simply place the drip pan items into the pan that you have been using the whole time. If there is an excessive amount of fatty drippings, either remove and replace the drip pan or use a turkey baster to remove the bulk of the drippings. Drip pan cooking should benefit from the natural flavors falling from above and not be swamped with too much oil and fat.

Our drip pan recipes include an estimated cooking time to get these dishes cooked through. Compare the cooking time of the main course with these recipes and add the drip pan items when necessary so that both dishes are done at the same time. If need be, drip pan items can be kept warm in the oven set to a low temperature.

Brazilian Pineapple

1 large pineapple

Rub

2 tablespoons (25 g) sugar

2 tablespoons (30 g) packed brown sugar

1 teaspoon ground cinnamon

½ teaspoon ground cloves

¼ teaspoon ground allspice

1 to 2 tablespoons (15 to 30 ml) rum (optional)

Yield: 4 to 6 servings

This is a fantastic pineapple recipe that can be served as a side dish, as dessert, or chopped and added to salsas. While most pineapple recipes call for the addition of rum or tequila, the Brazilian method does not. If you are so inclined to add spirits, do so after it has cooked. We've found that a little splash (1 to 2 tablespoons, or 15 to 30 ml) of rum after the pineapple has been cooked and chopped really does the trick. Otherwise, it's perfectly delicious without it.

1. Prepare the grill for medium, direct heat.

2. Cut the crown and bottom from the pineapple and, with it standing on the cut end, trim away the skin, making sure to remove all the dark brown bits.

3. Leave the core in place, run a long sword skewer through the center of the pineapple lengthwise to create a pilot hole, and thread the rotisserie rod through. Secure with the forks.

4. To make the rub: Combine the rub ingredients in a small bowl and apply all over the pineapple.

5. Place the pineapple on the preheated grill and set a drip pan underneath. Cook the pineapple for 10 to 12 minutes. It will become far too overcooked after this point. Remove from the grill and place on a cutting board. Let the pineapple cool for about 3 to 4 minutes, then carefully remove the rotisserie forks and slide the rod out.

6. Slice the pineapple into quarters vertically. Cut along the center of each piece to remove the core. Cut each quarter into bite-size pieces. At this point, you can add a little rum to the pineapple pieces, if using. Toss to coat and serve.

DRIP PAN POTATOES WITH LEMON

5 large yellow potatoes

1 tablespoon (15 ml) olive oil

½ teaspoon salt, plus more as needed

¼ teaspoon freshly ground black pepper

Juice of 1 large lemon

Yield: 4 servings

This is arguably the perfect side dish for any rotisserie chicken. The lemon juice brightens the flavors of these potatoes and the drippings provide the right amount of savoriness. We always make this dish with our Oregano Chicken (page 148), but to be honest, this dish works well with most of the chicken, turkey, and prime rib recipes. It is key to monitor the pan for excess fat from the drippings. If this becomes an issue, simply drain off any excess into a disposable jar or sturdy container and resume cooking.

1. Rinse the potatoes well, dry, and cut into 1½-inch (3.8 cm) pieces. Place in a drip pan, add the oil, salt, and pepper and toss to coat.

2. During the last half of the cooking time for the roast, remove the existing drip pan under the roast and set aside (either salvage enough for a gravy or discard completely). Place the pan with the potatoes under the roast and cook for 35 to 45 minutes, or until tender. If too much fat is released into the pan, use a turkey baster to remove excess.

3. Ideally, the roast and the potatoes will be done at the same time. Chicken cooks much faster, so add the pan underneath after 15 to 20 minutes of cooking time.

4. Remove the pan with the potatoes and sprinkle with the fresh lemon juice. Gently toss to coat. Taste for salt and add more if needed and serve. If the meat is resting, cover the pan with aluminum foil and serve once the chicken or beef is sliced.

Drip Pan Squash Medley

1 medium acorn squash

1 medium butternut squash

½ teaspoon salt,
plus more as needed

¼ teaspoon freshly ground
black pepper, plus more
as needed

¼ cup (60 ml) water

Yield: 6 servings

Acorn and butternut squash need time to cook, which makes them perfect for a drip pan dish. They have time to pick up all the flavors and slow roast. There is water in this recipe and it is a good idea to keep an eye on that during the cooking time. If the pan runs dry, add more hot water so that the squash has something to cook in.

1. Slice each squash in half. Scoop out the seeds and cut the squash into ½-inch (1.3 cm) slices with the skin on. You can peel the skin off before slicing if you prefer. Place in a drip pan and season with the salt and pepper. Carefully pour the water into the bottom of the pan around the squash.

2. After the roast has been on for 30 minutes to 1 hour (or chicken for 15 to 20 minutes), place the pan with the squash underneath the roast. Cook for 40 to 45 minutes. Drain the pan of excess fat and return it to the grill for 15 more minutes. Add more salt, pepper, and water, if needed.

3. Remove the squash from the heat. Transfer to a large platter and serve.

Drip Pan Bacon-Wrapped Brussels Sprouts

2 pounds (910 g)
Brussels sprouts

1 (1-pound, or 454 g)
package thick-cut bacon

Yield: 4 to 6 servings

The key to this Brussels sprout dish is not to overcook them. Remember that less is more when it comes to this vegetable. They should be tender, but still have a little bite to them. Wrapped in bacon, these Brussels sprouts will be loved even by people who normally don't like them. Given that this is a drip pan recipe, the bacon will cook beautifully, but will not be overly crispy.

1. Wash the Brussels sprouts and pat dry with paper towels.

2. Cut strips of bacon into halves or thirds and wrap each sprout with a piece of bacon. Make sure the strips of bacon overlap the sprout. Secure with 1 or 2 toothpicks and place in the drip pan.

3. During the last 25 to 30 minutes of the roast or poultry's cooking time, remove the existing drip pan. Scoop out 2 tablespoons (30 ml) of drippings and drizzle over the bacon-wrapped sprouts. Place the pan directly under the meat and cook for 20 to 25 minutes, or until the bacon has cooked though and the sprouts are tender but not mushy. Remove the pan and the roast from the grill.

4. While the meat is resting, remove the cooked sprouts from the pan and transfer to a platter. Remove the toothpicks and serve along with the main dish.

Drip Pan Carrots

8 to 10 large carrots

1 large onion, cut into chunks

1 tablespoon (15 ml)
balsamic vinegar

¼ teaspoon salt

¼ teaspoon freshly ground
black pepper

Yield: 6 servings

Why bake or sauté carrots when they can be prepared right on the grill along with a flavorful roast, chicken, or turkey? This recipe is simple but convenient and equally as delicious.

1. Wash the carrots well and pat dry with paper towels. Either peel the carrots or leave the cleaned skins on. Chop into ¾-inch (2 cm) diagonal slices. Place the carrots and the onion chunks in a drip pan and season with the balsamic vinegar, salt, and pepper.

2. Remove the existing drip pan from under the roast and spoon out 2 to 3 tablespoons (20 to 45 ml) of drippings. Add to the carrots and toss well to coat. Place on the grill under the roast or poultry during the last 25 to 30 minutes of cooking time. Cook until tender but not mushy.

3. Remove from the grill along with the cooked meat. Cover the pan to keep warm. Serve as a side.

Drip Pan Asparagus and Garlic

3 pounds (1.4 kg) asparagus, washed and trimmed

4 cloves garlic, thinly sliced

2 teaspoons olive oil

½ teaspoon salt

¼ teaspoon freshly ground black pepper

Juice of 1 lemon

Yield: 6 to 8 servings

If you're a fan of asparagus and looking for a quick method for preparing it on the grill, then this recipe is for you. Be sure to choose a neutral-flavored beef, pork, or poultry item as the drippings source.

1. Combine the asparagus, garlic, oil, salt, and pepper in a large bowl and toss to coat. Add to the drip pan set under the rotisserie roast or poultry during the last 25 minutes of cooking time. Cook for 20 to 25 minutes, tossing with tongs every 5 minutes or so. Watch for burning. If you are using a particularly fatty cut of meat, remove some drippings from the pan with a turkey baster.

2. The asparagus should be toothsome and not overcooked when done. Remove right away along with the roast. Keep warm until ready to serve. The asparagus will continue to soften a bit by the time the roast or poultry is ready to carve. Squeeze the fresh lemon juice over the top right before serving.

DRIP PAN BROCCOLI

2 heads broccoli, cut into large florets

Zest and juice of 1 lemon

1 teaspoon olive oil

¼ teaspoon salt

¼ teaspoon red pepper flakes

Yield: 4 to 6 servings

This recipe really takes that boring old steamed broccoli up a notch. There is nothing like the drippings of roasted beef or rotisserie chicken to really help flavor vegetables. The more complex the flavor of the main dish, the better. We recommend the Spanish Paprika Chicken (page 150) or the Balsamic-Glazed Chuck Roast (page 87) for this dish.

1. Place all the ingredients in a drip pan and toss to coat the broccoli florets.

2. Time it so that you are putting the broccoli under the roast during the last 25 to 30 minutes of cooking. Remove the previous drip pan from under the roast. Scoop out 1 to 2 tablespoons (15 to 30 ml) of drippings and drizzle over the broccoli. Set the broccoli pan under the roast and cook for 25 to 30 minutes, tossing with tongs every 5 minutes or so.

3. Remove the drip pan and the roast at the same time. Keep warm until ready to serve.

TUMBLE BASKET POTATOES

2½ to 3 pounds (1.2 to 1.4 kg) medium-size red or new potatoes

3 tablespoons (45 ml) olive oil

2½ teaspoons salt

½ teaspoon freshly ground black pepper

Butter Sauce

¼ cup (55 g) unsalted butter, melted

2 tablespoons (30 ml) olive oil

1 small shallot, finely chopped

1 teaspoon roughly chopped fresh thyme

¼ teaspoon salt

Yield: 4 to 6 servings

Here's a quick and easy recipe for rotisserie-style potatoes. The movement of the tumble basket actually helps fluff up the potatoes. We don't mean that the potatoes will be smashed like crazy—they will remain firm and intact—but they'll have a fluffier quality to them. After they are cooked, these potatoes are bathed in a silky butter sauce. Absolutely delicious.

1. Prepare the grill for medium-high heat with indirect cooking.

2. Rinse the potatoes and pat dry with paper towels. Place in a large bowl along with oil, salt, and pepper. Toss to coat, transfer to a tumble basket, and secure.

3. Place the tumble basket on the grill and cook the potatoes for 35 to 45 minutes, or until tender. Test with a knife. If it pierces easily and flows toward the center without any resistance, then the potatoes are done.

4. Remove the basket from the grill and carefully transfer the potatoes to a large serving bowl. Cover with aluminum foil to keep warm.

5. To make the butter sauce: Combine all the sauce ingredients in a small bowl. Pour the butter mixture over the potatoes and toss to coat. Serve.

Drip Pan Beets

6 large beets, peeled and chopped into 1½-inch (3.8 cm) pieces

1 tablespoon (15 ml) olive oil

Juice of 2 large limes, divided

½ teaspoon salt, plus more as needed

½ teaspoon white pepper

Yield: 8 servings

Typically, beets are not cooked well. They lack flavor and are too bland. We like beets cooked in a charcoal grill with a good dose of smoke so they get all that extra flavor (see page 22). A good beef roast rotating over the top does not hurt either.

1. Place the chopped beets into a drip pan, add the oil, the juice of 1 lime, and the salt and pepper, and toss to coat.

2. Remove the drip pan already under the roast and set aside. If cooking a rib roast, place the beets underneath during the last 45 minutes to 1 hour of cooking time. If cooking a chicken, place the pan underneath after the first 15 minutes of cooking time.

3. Cook the beets for 45 to 55 minutes, or until nice and tender. If the roast produces too much fat (this happens with rib roast), drain the pan or use a turkey baster to remove most of the fat. However, leave a little behind.

4. Once the beets have cooked through, remove the pan from the grill and drizzle with the remaining lime juice. Taste for salt and add more if needed. Gently toss to coat and serve.

DRIP PAN MUSHROOMS

1 pound (454 g) cremini or
white mushrooms, cleaned

1 tablespoon (15 ml) olive oil

½ teaspoon salt

½ teaspoon freshly
ground black pepper

2 tablespoons (8 g) chopped
flat-leaf parsley

Yield: 4 to 6 servings

This is our favorite, fast side dish for beef roasts. Because these mushrooms only take about 30 minutes (or less, depending on your grill and grilling configuration), we simply swap this drip pan with the one that we were using. When the roast comes off the grill, the mushrooms are ready. Seal the pan with aluminum foil and keep it warm until the meat has rested.

1. In a drip pan, combine the mushrooms with the oil, salt, and pepper. Toss to coat.

2. During the last 30 to 35 minutes of cooking time, remove the drip pan from under the roast (use for gravy or discard) and replace with the mushroom pan. Cook for about 30 minutes.

3. Remove the pan from the heat and remove any excess fat with a spoon or turkey baster. Transfer to a serving dish and top with the chopped parsley.

CHILI-LIME ROTISSERIE CAULIFLOWER

1 whole cauliflower,
about 2 pounds (910 g)

Rub

¼ cup (60 ml) olive oil

½ teaspoon salt

½ teaspoon onion powder

½ teaspoon ground cumin

½ teaspoon chili powder

½ teaspoon dried oregano

¼ teaspoon garlic powder or 1
clove garlic, minced

¼ teaspoon freshly
ground black pepper

Baste

Juice of 2 large limes

2 tablespoons (30 ml) olive oil,
plus more for drizzling

½ teaspoon rub mixture

¼ cup (4 g) chopped
fresh cilantro or
2 tablespoons (2 g)
chopped fresh chives,
for garnish

Yield: 4 to 6 servings

Boiled cauliflower is awful. It really is. Roasted cauliflower is something entirely different. It has all the flavor without the bitterness, and by grilling it we get so much more out of it. For a couple of people who do not really like cauliflower, this has become one of our favorite vegetable side dishes. Trust us. You really have to try it. And once you do, you can double this recipe by threading two heads onto the rotisserie, stem end to stem end.

---

1. Prepare the grill for medium-high heat with indirect cooking.

2. Cut away any long leaves from the cauliflower, but keep most of the green and stem intact. Run a long sword skewer through the center of the cauliflower lengthwise to create a pilot hole. Gently work the rotisserie rod through the center and secure with the forks.

3. To make the rub: Combine the rub ingredients in a small bowl and reserve ½ teaspoon for the baste. Apply the remaining rub all over the cauliflower, rotating to reach the entire surface.

4. To make the baste: Combine the baste ingredients in a small bowl and set aside.

5. Place the cauliflower on the preheated grill and cook for 35 to 40 minutes. Begin basting the cauliflower after the first 15 to 20 minutes of cooking time. Do this every 5 to 8 minutes, or until the cauliflower is nice and tender.

6. Remove from the grill and let the cauliflower cool for 3 to 5 minutes before handling. Carefully remove the rotisserie forks and slide the rod out, and then set the cauliflower on a large cutting board. Cut off the stem and slice or cut the cauliflower into smaller florets. Drizzle with olive oil, top with the chopped cilantro, and serve.

CAULIFLOWER STEAKS

2 medium heads cauliflower

Rub

1½ tablespoons (23 ml) olive oil

2 teaspoons balsamic vinegar

½ teaspoon salt, plus more as needed

½ teaspoon sweet paprika

½ teaspoon dried oregano

¼ teaspoon garlic powder

¼ teaspoon freshly ground black pepper

Yield: 4 or 5 servings

You'll need a flat basket, a good sharp serrated knife, and a little patience for this recipe. Cauliflower tends to break apart as you cut it, so purchasing two is a good idea. If you're left with smaller florets and scraps, simply store those in the fridge or freezer to add to soups and stir-fries. These cauliflower steaks are seasoned in a delicious balsamic rub and cooked for a short amount of time on the grill. You can serve them as a side dish or add to tacos, pasta, or salads.

1. Prepare the grill for medium-high heat with indirect cooking.

2. Wash the cauliflower heads and pat dry with paper towels. Remove the leaves, but keep the stems intact. Cut into ½- to ¾-inch (1.3 to 2 cm) vertical slabs. Some smaller pieces will fall away. Move those aside. You should end up with 6 to 8 steaks.

3. To make the rub: Combine the rub ingredients in a small bowl. Taste for salt and add more if needed. Rub the mixture onto one side of the steaks, carefully place in a flat basket, and secure.

4. Place the flat basket on the rotisserie unit and cook the cauliflower for 20 minutes. It should be tender but still have a lot of texture. Remove from the grill and carefully remove from the basket. Transfer to a platter and serve.

TUMBLE BASKET CORN

6 to 8 ears fresh corn

Olive oil,
for brushing the corn

Yield: 6 to 8 servings

This is one of the easiest ways to prepare corn on the grill. It's fast enough that if you have a roast that needs a 15- to 20-minute rest time, the corn will be done in time to carve the meat. This recipe has two ingredients, but feel free to serve with softened butter and Parmesan cheese on the side, or your favorite toppings. Your tumble basket might not be large enough to accommodate 8 large ears of corn, so determine the capacity before you start.

1. Prepare the grill for medium-high heat with indirect cooking.

2. Husk the corn and remove the silks. Cut 1 inch (2.5 cm) off the top of each ear, removing the point. Brush with oil, place in the tumble basket, and secure.

3. Place the basket on the preheated grill and cook over medium-high heat for 15 to 20 minutes. Remove from the grill and transfer to a large platter. Serve with your favorite flavorings.

Acknowledgments

Rotisserie cooking has always been something we have enjoyed doing and we have long advocated its inherent benefits. It goes without saying that writing an entire cookbook on the subject tested both our creative abilities and our grilling skills. Many have offered indispensible advice, ideas, and techniques that made this process quite rewarding. Friends and family served as taste testers during the recipe development phase, and we thank them for all of their feedback, compliments, and criticisms that helped to shape this book into its final form.

Dan Rosenberg of Harvard Common Press introduced this topic and helped steer it from concept to publication calmly and carefully. Anne Re and Renae Haines at Harvard Common Press did a masterful job of handling the layout and production, and Karen Levy made sure that the text was properly edited and actually made sense. Mark and Mary Beth Maziarz did a fantastic job with the food styling and photography.

Will Wilson at Snider Bros Meats patiently dug through meat cases and the back room to find perfect cuts. He offered invaluable advice that only a knowledgeable butcher can. The owners and employees at Beltex Meats assisted us in finding and obtaining more complicated cuts of meat. Countless manufacturers, inventors, and suppliers have filled our patio, garage, and basement with test products, prototypes, and demonstration units over the years. This in itself made out job so much easier by allowing us to test these recipes on every conceivable style and type of grill.

And, innumerable thanks are owed to the legions of online readers over the years whose questions and comments have challenged everything we ever thought we knew about outdoor cooking.

About the Authors

DERRICK RICHES has served as the barbecue and grilling expert at TheSpruce.com for the last two decades. As one of the most popular destinations for outdoor cooking information, he has answered thousands of questions, written hundreds of articles, and explored barbecue in its widest definition. During this time he has traveled the world, grilled on almost every conceivable kind of cooking equipment, and judged the best barbecue in the world.

SABRINA BAKSH is a recipe developer, editor, food stylist, and food photographer whose work has been published in a variety of online and print venues. She has traveled the world exploring flavors, cultures, and food history.

Index

Kebabs
978-1-55832-872-3

25 Essentials:
Techniques for Planking
978-1-55832-877-8

25 Essentials:
Techniques for Smoking
978-1-55832-878-5

25 Essentials:
Wood-Fired Ovens
978-1-55832-885-3